American Book Company
The Standards Experts

MASTERING THE
GEORGIA 5TH GRADE CRCT
IN
ENGLISH LANGUAGE ARTS

Mallory Grantham

Sara Hinton

Project Coordinator: Zuzana Urbanek
Executive Editor: Dr. Frank J. Pintozzi

American Book Company
PO Box 2638
Woodstock, GA 30188-1383
Toll Free: 1 (888) 264-5877 Phone: (770) 928-2834
Fax: (770) 928-7483 Toll Free Fax: 1 (866) 827-3240
www.americanbookcompany.com

ACKNOWLEDGEMENTS

We would like to gratefully acknowledge the formatting and technical contributions of Marsha Torrens and Becky Wright as well as the writing contributions of Jason Kirk.

We also appreciate the proofreading expertise of Susan Barrows.

Table of Contents

Chapter 7   Writing Essays   83

Chapter 8   Research   95

Practice Test 1   107

Practice Test 2   125

Index   143

Preface

Mastering the Georgia 5th Grade CRCT in English Language Arts will help students who are reviewing for the grade 5 CRCT in English Language Arts. The materials in this book are based on the Georgia GPS standards and other materials published by the Georgia Department of Education. This book is written to the grade 5 reading level and corresponds to 750L to 950L on the Lexile text measure scale.

This book contains the following sections:

1) General information about the book

2) A diagnostic test

3) A diagnostic evaluation chart

4) Eight chapters that teach the concepts and skills needed for test readiness

5) Two practice tests

Standards are posted at the beginning of each chapter and section review, and they are matched to each question in the diagnostic and practice tests. A chart of standards is included in the teacher's answer manual.

We welcome comments and suggestions about the book. Please contact the authors at

American Book Company
PO Box 2638
Woodstock, GA 30188-1383

Toll Free: 1 (888) 264-5877
Phone: (770) 928-2834
Fax: (770) 928-7483
Web site: www.americanbookcompany.com

About the Authors

Mallory Grantham is an ELA writer and copy editor at American Book Company. She completed her Bachelor of Arts in English at Kennesaw State University. As a teaching assistant, she led lectures, created lesson plans, graded and edited papers, and evaluated student progress. In addition, Mallory has taught sign language and tutored students in English and mathematics.

Sara Hinton has a B.A. from Columbia University and an M.A. in the teaching of English from Teachers College, Columbia University. She taught middle school language arts and college courses in writing, grammar, and literature for several years.

About the Project Coordinator: **Zuzana Urbanek** serves as ELA Curriculum Coordinator for American Book Company. She is a professional writer with twenty-five years of experience in education, business, and publishing. She has taught a variety of English courses since 1990 at the college level and also taught English as a foreign language abroad. Her master's degree is from Arizona State University.

About the Executive Editor: **Dr. Frank J. Pintozzi** is a former Professor of Education at Kennesaw State University. For over twenty-eight years, he has taught English and reading at the high school and college levels as well as in teacher preparation courses in language arts and social studies. In addition to writing and editing state standard-specific texts for high school exit and end-of-course exams, he has edited and written several college textbooks.

GA 5 CRCT ELA
Diagnostic Test

The purpose of this diagnostic test is to evaluate your skills in a variety of areas linked to the grade 5 English Language Arts standards published by the Georgia Department of Education.

This test is set up in two sections, like the actual CRCT. When you take the CRCT, you have forty-five to seventy minutes to complete each section, with a ten-minute break between them.

GENERAL DIRECTIONS

1 **Read all directions carefully.**

2 **Read each selection.**

3 **Read each question or example. Then, choose the best answer.**

4 **Choose only one answer for each question. If you change an answer, be sure to erase the answer completely.**

5 **At the end of the test, you or your instructor should score your test. Using the evaluation chart following the test, determine whether or not you are prepared for the reading and research skills tested on the fifth-grade CRCT in English Language Arts.**

Section 1

1   **What part of speech is the underlined word in the sentence?**   5C1a

> Markus and Jenna worked on a <u>science</u> project together and won a ribbon at the fair!

A   noun

B   adjective

C   conjunction

D   interjection

2   **What kind of sentence is this?**   5C1e

> Before I opened my presents, I thanked everyone for coming to my party.

A   simple

B   compound

C   complex

D   compound-complex

3   **What part of speech is the underlined word in the sentence?**   5C1a

> The Internet lets people look up information quickly and <u>easily</u>.

A   adverb

B   adjective

C   interjection

D   pronoun

4   **What is the BEST way to combine these sentences?**   5C1b

> I have two apples. Megan also has two. Tripp has one.

A   I have two apples; Megan also has two, but Tripp has one.

B   Megan and I have two apples each, while Tripp has one.

C   Me and Megan have two apples, and Tripp has one apple.

D   I have two apples and so does Megan, and Tripp has one.

5 **Which verb phrase BEST completes the sentence?**   5C1c

> Because the factory closed last year, all the workers _____ away.

A   is moving

B   are moved

C   has been moved

D   have been moving

6 **Which of these is a complete sentence?**   5C1f

A   He likes cookies fresh from the oven.

B   But not the cream-filled kind.

C   Because they are usually too sweet.

D   He and Julia, who loves chocolate.

7 **What part of speech is the underlined word in the sentence?**   5C1a

> On weekends, Trey volunteers at the animal shelter where his family <u>adopted</u> a cat.

A   adjective

B   adverb

C   verb

D   noun

8 **The following paragraph is an example of what organizational structure?**   5W1c

> Martha has two pets. One is a Jack Russell terrier puppy named Roscoe. He is white with brown patches on his eyes. He likes to play and run in the yard. He is two years old. Her other pet is a Siamese cat named Lina. She is also two years old. Lina is gray with pointy ears, and she would rather sleep under Martha's bed than play outside. Roscoe and Lina are very different animals, but Martha loves them both very much.

A   cause and effect

B   chronological order

C   question and answer

D   compare and contrast

9 If Martha was going to write a science report about her Jack Russell terrier, which reference source would be the BEST to use?   5W3c

   A   a book about different dog breeds

   B   a newspaper ad selling a dog

   C   an Internet article about training dogs

   D   a magazine for dog lovers

10   Which sentence uses *state* as a noun?   5C1d

   A   Ricardo is going to the state fair this weekend.

   B   Would you please state your name and age?

   C   My best friend is moving to another state.

   D   Polly's class is visiting the state capitol today.

11   Which verb phrase BEST completes the sentence?   5C1c

Naya _____ to be chosen as the soloist in the Christmas pageant.

   A   honors

   B   honored

   C   is honoring

   D   was honored

12   Which sentence uses an apostrophe correctly?   5C1g

   A   My brother eat's so much food!

   B   Jillian's sister is very pretty.

   C   A hamster is very protective of it's young.

   D   Ivan could'nt understand the foreign movie.

13 Which sentence in the paragraph below repeats an idea?   5W2

> [1]I love all types of flowers. [2]Roses are my favorite kind. [3]Their scent is very fragrant. [4]They smell beautiful. [5]Daisies are fun because they come in many colors. [6]Tulips remind me of spring, but poinsettias remind me of Christmas.

A   sentence 1

B   sentence 2

C   sentence 4

D   sentence 5

14 Which is the BEST closing sentence for the paragraph below?   5W2

> Dexter was furious with himself. He had finished his science project, written a nice report, and decorated a nice poster. He had worked very hard. In fact, poor Dexter had been working so hard on his project that he had forgotten the most difficult part—the presentation. The presentation part would be the worst because Dexter had a fear of speaking in front of others, especially when those others were his classmates.

A   Dexter thought speeches were dumb.

B   He was not looking forward to class now.

C   He shouldn't have worked so hard.

D   Dexter's teacher gave him extra credit.

15 What type of sentence is this?   5C1e

> We just won the state championship!

A   declarative

B   imperative

C   exclamatory

D   interrogative

16 Which of these sentences is a run-on? 5C1f

   A When Opal saw the snake, she screamed.

   B Quinn ran to Ray's house, they played marbles.

   C Kevin studied very hard for his test; he tried his best.

   D Mrs. Johnston gave us a pop quiz this morning.

17 What is the BEST way to correct this sentence? 5C1b

> Two cars were reported stolen by the Farmingdale police yesterday.

   A Yesterday, two cars were reported stolen by the Farmingdale police.

   B Two cars by the Farmingdale police were reported stolen yesterday.

   C Two cars were reported yesterday stolen by the Farmingdale police.

   D Yesterday, the Farmingdale police reported that two cars were stolen.

18 Which transition would BEST connect the two sentences? 5W1d

> Trent was determined to finish the puzzle. His mom told him it was time for bed.

   A so

   B and

   C however

   D consequently

19 Which is the BEST topic sentence for the paragraph below? 5W2

> There is always shopping to do, because gift-giving is important to many people. Lots of people have family over to celebrate. That means cooking and baking and preparing. Sometimes, it can be stressful, but the spirit of the holidays usually keeps people in a good mood.

   A The holiday season is a busy time for many people.

   B There's a lot of things to do this time of year.

   C Some people ignore the upcoming holiday season.

   D I am never busy during the holiday season.

20 What part of speech is the underlined word in the sentence?   5C1a

> Vince <u>convinced</u> his father to let him ride the go-karts.

A adjective

B noun

C verb

D pronoun

21 Which word would BEST complete this sentence?   5C1g

> You'll call me if _____ is any news, right?

A they're

B there

C their

D thare

22 Which word would BEST replace the underlined word in the sentence?   5W3g

> Ria's grandfather is a <u>weathered</u> actor; he's been in the business a long time.

A veteran

B tested

C novice

D tense

23 The following paragraph is an example of what organizational structure?   5W1c

> Ida had a birthday party today. All of her friends came over. They ate pizza and played games outside. Then, Ida opened her presents. She loved all of her gifts. Cake and ice cream finished the perfect afternoon.

A cause and effect

B compare and contrast

C question and answer

D chronological order

24 **Which transition would BEST connect the two sentences?**   5W1d

Emma is a very clean person. Sean keeps his room messy.

A   and

B   while

C   because

D   since

25 **Which verb phrase BEST completes the sentence?**   5C1c

Since it rained today, Julian _____ a rainbow.

A   could saw

B   can seeing

C   could see

D   can saw

26 **What type of sentence is this?**   5C1e

Please empty your dirty clothes hamper.

A   declarative

B   imperative

C   exclamatory

D   interrogative

27 Which sentence in the paragraph below repeats an idea?   5W2

> [1]Stella and Nina are making homemade cards today. [2]They are making cards for their grandmother. [3]Her birthday is coming up soon. [4]They want to make her day very special. [5]They draw pretty pictures and add glitter and bright colors. [6]Stella and Nina know their grandmother will love the cards.

A sentence 2

B sentence 4

C sentence 5

D sentence 6

28 Which supporting detail is MOST important to add to the paragraph above?   5W2

A Stella's picture is prettier than Nina's picture.

B Nina drew flowers on her picture, and Stella drew a horse.

C Stella wants to play hopscotch later, but Nina likes to draw.

D Nina is older than Stella by two years.

29 Which word would BEST replace the underlined word in the sentence?   5W4b

> Evan got his braces off yesterday; his smile is <u>blazing</u>.

A scorching

B glittery

C flaming

D dazzling

30 What is the BEST way to combine these sentences?   5C1b

> Uriah visited his uncle and aunt over the summer. He visited them in Arkansas.

A Uriah visited his uncle and aunt over the summer; he visited in Arkansas.

B Uriah visited his uncle and aunt over the summer, and he went to Arkansas.

C Uriah visited his uncle and aunt in Arkansas over the summer.

D Uriah visited Arkansas and his uncle and aunt over the summer.

Section 2

31 **What part of speech is the underlined word in the sentence?**   5C1a

> Kaitlin always does her homework as soon as she gets <u>home</u>.

A adverb

B adjective

C noun

D verb

32 **What is the BEST way to combine these sentences?**   5C1b

> It started raining. We ran the rest of the way home.

A Because it started raining, we ran the rest of the way home.

B Before we ran the rest of the way home, it started raining.

C We ran, because it started raining, the rest of the way home.

D It started raining, although we ran the rest of the way home.

33 **What part of speech is the underlined word in the sentence?**   5C1a

> How did you get that huge piano <u>through</u> the front door?

A verb

B conjunction

C pronoun

D preposition

34 **Which sentence has the correct punctuation?**   5C1f

A I'd love to visit Australia it has the most interesting animals.

B My Uncle Luke visited Australia, and he brought me a boomerang.

C Marsupials live there, they have pouches where they carry their babies.

D Wallabies and kangaroos, look similar, but are different animals.

35 **Which transition would BEST connect the two sentences?** 5W1d

> Renee is studying for her history test. She would rather be playing outside.

A and

B although

C consequently

D since

36 **Which is the BEST topic sentence for the paragraph below?** 5W2

> But just how much work is it to plan a party? First, you have to invite people to come, which means buying invitations or calling everyone. You also need to have some kind of refreshments. It is important to have some form of entertainment. That could be anything from karaoke to watching movies to playing video games. It doesn't matter who you invite, what you eat, or what you do, what is important is to have fun!

A Planning a party can be fun, but it can be a lot of hard work.

B Parties are a good way to become popular.

C Everyone has an idea of what a perfect party should be like.

D What is your favorite event to throw a party for?

37 **The paragraph above is an example of what organizational structure?** 5W1a

A cause and effect

B chronological order

C question and answer

D compare and contrast

38 **Which verb phrase BEST completes the sentence?** 5C1c

> Author John Steinbeck _____ the novel *Cannery Row* in 1945.

A is writing

B wrote

C has written

D writes

39 Which sentence uses quotation marks correctly?   5C1g

    A Where is the committee meeting? "David asked."

    B Where is the "committee meeting"? David asked.

    C "Where is the committee meeting? David asked."

    (D) "Where is the committee meeting?" David asked.

40 What part of speech is the underlined word in this sentence?   5C1a

> I am writing this letter to ask for <u>information</u>.

    A verb

    (B) adverb

    C noun

    D pronoun

41 What kind of sentence is this?   5C1e

> Even though it rained heavily, Molly had taken her umbrella, so she did not get very wet.

    A simple

    B complex

    C compound

    (D) compound-complex

42 Which sentence in the paragraph below repeats an idea?   5W2

> [1]I love the springtime. [2]The rain makes everything grow. [3]The colors of the earth are beautiful. [4]The flowers bloom, and all the animals come out from hibernation. [5]I love how the rain causes the plants to grow. [6]Spring is the best season.

    A sentence 1

    B sentence 3

    (C) sentence 4

    D sentence 5

43 Which sentence from the previous paragraph is written in first-person point of view?

5W2

A I love the springtime.

B The rain makes everything grow.

C The colors of the earth are beautiful.

D Spring is the best season.

44 Which word would BEST complete this sentence?

5C1g

> "Grab _____ bag, and we'll leave right now," he said.

A you're

B your

C youre

D yore

45 What is the BEST way to correct this sentence?

5C1b

> The cowboy was thrown by the bull in a leather vest.

A The cowboy in a leather vest was thrown by the bull.

B The cowboy in a leather vest was threw the bull.

C In a leather vest, the bull threw the cowboy.

D The cowboy threw the bull in a leather vest.

46 Which of these sentences is a fragment?

5C1f

A I found a rat in the basement.

B He hopped on his bike.

C The police officer was friendly.

D Randy in the house next door.

47 **Which transition would BEST connect the ideas in this sentence?** 5W1d

> Isla decided to take sewing lessons _____ she twisted her ankle and couldn't play sports.

A and

B yet

C because

D although

48 **The following paragraph is an example of what organizational structure?** 5W1c

> Giana wanted to make her mom a birthday cake. She got out the ingredients she needed: eggs, flour, butter, and sugar. She read the directions very carefully. She mixed the batter and poured it into two circle pans. Her dad put them into the oven. Giana waited patiently for the cakes to finish.

A cause and effect

B chronological order

C question and answer

D similarity and difference

49 **If Giana was going to look for another cake recipe, what would be the BEST source for her to look at?** 5W3c

A a newspaper ad selling an oven

B an Internet article about cooking healthy foods

C an encyclopedia article about the history of cake

D a cookbook with desserts

50 **What part of speech is the underlined word in the sentence?** 5C1a

> "Well, I think we should eat pizza tonight since we had Chinese yesterday," Mario said.

A adjective

B adverb

C interjection

D preposition

51 What kind of sentence is this?   5C1e

> Jeremy was in charge of making nachos, and Nancy chopped the onions.

A simple

B compound

C complex

D compound-complex

52 Which sentence in the paragraph below repeats an idea?   5W2

> [1]The football players train hard by running laps and making plays. [2]The football players want to win the game. [3]They throw the ball and tackle each other. [4]Their coach yells at them, but it makes them practice harder. [5]They have to practice to win the game. [6]Their game is on Friday.

A sentence 1

B sentence 2

C sentence 4

D sentence 6

53 Which supporting detail is MOST important to add to the paragraph above?   5W2

A The quarterback is taller than any player on the team.

B The punter has a broken toe so he cannot play.

C Each player is prepared to play their best on Friday.

D The coach is retiring after this year.

54 Which word would BEST replace the underlined word in the sentence?   5W4b

> Uri and Carey don't really dislike each other; they just pretend to <u>attack</u>.

A argue

B tussle

C dispute

D banter

55 **What is the BEST way to combine these sentences?**   5C1b

> Erin loves to rollerblade. Her father takes her to the local skate park.

A   Erin loves to rollerblade, her father takes her to the local skate park.

B   Erin loves to rollerblade so her father takes her to the local skate park.

C   Erin loves to rollerblade; and her father takes her to the local skate park.

D   Erin loves to rollerblade, but her father takes her to the local skate park.

56 **Which sentence uses a colon correctly?**   5C1g

A   Vera needs to: finish her homework, do her chores, and eat dinner.

B   Please bring: ice cream, soda, and chips to the party tomorrow.

C   Kyle wants to play the following sports: baseball and tennis.

D   Paula and Wilma are best friends and have been since: kindergarten.

57 **Which verb phrase BEST completes the sentence?**   5C1c

> Stephanie _____ married next week.

A   is getting

B   was getting

C   has gotten

D   had gotten

58 **Which of these is a run-on?**   5C1f

A   Noah did not know when his cousin was visiting.

B   Rachel tried, but she could not see the parade.

C   Kurt is responsible; he turns in his work on time.

D   Tina has to cook dinner, her mom works late.

59 **What part of speech is the underlined word in the sentence?** 5C1a

> Bailey plays the drums in his <u>school</u> band.

A adverb

B adjective

C interjection

D pronoun

60 **The sentence below is written in what point of view?** 5W2

> If you study hard and do your work, you can get good grades too!

A first person

B second person

C third person

D It does not have a point of view.

EVALUATION CHART FOR GEORGIA 5TH GRADE CRCT IN ENGLISH LANGUAGE ARTS DIAGNOSTIC TEST

Directions: On the following chart, circle the question numbers that you answered incorrectly and evaluate the results. Then turn to the appropriate chapters, read the explanations, and complete the exercises. Review other chapters as needed. Finally, complete the practice tests to assess your progress and further prepare you for the **Georgia 5th Grade CRCT in ELA**.

Note: Some question numbers will appear under multiple chapters because those questions require demonstration of multiple skills.

Chapters	Diagnostic Test Questions
Chapter 1: Parts of Speech	1, 3, 7, 10, 20, 31, 33, 40, 50, 59
Chapter 2: Usage and Grammar	5, 11, 12, 21, 25, 38, 39, 44, 56, 57
Chapter 3: Punctuation	6, 12, 16, 34, 39, 44, 46, 56, 58
Chapter 4: Spelling	21, 44
Chapter 5: Working with Sentences	2, 4, 6, 15, 16, 17, 26, 30, 32, 34, 41, 45, 46, 51, 55, 58
Chapter 6: Working with Paragraphs	2, 4, 5, 8, 11, 13, 14, 15, 17, 18, 19, 23, 24, 25, 26, 27, 28, 29, 30, 32, 35, 36, 37, 38, 41, 42, 43, 45, 47, 48, 51, 52, 53, 54, 55, 57, 60
Chapter 7: Writing Essays	13, 14, 19, 27, 28, 29, 36, 42, 43, 52, 53, 54, 60
Chapter 8: Research	9, 13, 14, 19, 22, 27, 28, 29, 36, 42, 43, 49, 52, 53, 54, 60

Chapter 1
Parts of Speech

ENGLISH LANGUAGE ARTS

CRCT 5 5th GRADE

This chapter covers the following GPS-based CRCT standard:

ELA5C1 The student demonstrates understanding and control of the rules of the English language, realizing that usage involves the appropriate application of conventions and grammar in both written and spoken formats. The student	
a. Uses and identifies the eight parts of speech (e.g., noun, pronoun, verb, adverb, adjective, conjunction, preposition, interjection).	**d.** Recognizes that a word performs different functions according to its position in the sentence.

Parts of speech are the roles that words can play in a sentence.

A word like *play* can work as more than one part of speech. It can refer to a thing, as in "The drama club is putting on a <u>play</u>." Or it can be an action, as in "Derek and Marcy <u>play</u> tennis."

Do you know these two parts of speech? The first is a noun, and the second is a verb. Read on for more about parts of speech.

NOUNS

A **noun** is a person, place, or thing. Nouns are the subjects in most sentences, but not all nouns are subjects.

> **Example:** <u>Travis</u> and <u>Matt</u> played <u>football</u>.

In this sentence, *Travis*, *Matt*, and *football* are nouns. *Travis* and *Matt* are the subjects. *Football* is not the subject.

There are two kinds of nouns: **proper nouns** and **common nouns**. Proper nouns refer to specific things that have names. Common nouns refer to things that do not have individual names.

Proper nouns: Michelle, Pacific Ocean, Nikola Tesla, *Transformers*

Common nouns: neighbor, ocean, inventor, movie

PRONOUNS

A **pronoun** stands in for a noun. Writers and speakers use pronouns to avoid repeating a noun over and over.

This table shows pronouns that stand in for a few example nouns:

Noun:	Pronoun substitute:
J.K. Rowling	she
LeBron James and Shaquille O'Neal	they
father	he
computer	it
Carlita and I	we

Kinds of Pronouns		
Nominative	**Objective**	**Possessive**
I	me	my, mine
you	you	your, yours
she	her	her, hers
he	him	his
it	it	its
we	us	our, ours
they	them	their, theirs
who	whom	whose
whoever	whomever	

Practice 1: Nouns and Pronouns

1   **Which sentence uses <u>show</u> as a noun?**

   A   Show your boss how well you work.

   B   Tonight's show begins at 8 o'clock.

   C   The sun is finally starting to show.

   D   Let's show them what we're made of!

2   **Which pronoun could replace *Christina* in a sentence?**

   A   they   C   us

   B   our   D   she

3   Which sentence uses <u>start</u> as a noun?

   A At the start of the match, either player can win.

   B Start studying now if you want to pass.

   C It's time to start.

   D I didn't start baking the pies yet.

4   Which sentence does NOT use a pronoun?

   A I wiped down the counters before leaving for the night.

   B Walking the dogs was great until they all decided to run.

   C After the accident, Mike's car needs a pair of new wheels.

   D It looks like the game is over.

5   Which sentence does not use a noun?

   A Do you remember when they came to visit?

   B Red is my favorite color.

   C She had never seen anything like it in her town.

   D Tennessee is known for its hills and valleys.

VERBS

Verbs are action words. A **verb** shows what a person, place, or thing is doing.

Just as every sentence needs a subject, every sentence also needs a verb. The two work together to tell a small story. Imagine a sentence like "The cat jumped" without its noun or its verb. *Jumped* by itself isn't a complete thought, and neither is *the cat*.

Verbs must agree with the rest of the sentence. This means two things. A verb must agree with the subject it goes with, and it must agree with the overall tense of the sentence.

SUBJECT-VERB AGREEMENT

Singular subjects need singular verbs.

> **Example:** The <u>dolphin</u> <u>jumps</u> through the hoop.

Plural subjects need plural verbs.

> **Example:** The <u>dolphins</u> <u>jump</u> through the hoops.

Here's a rule that often applies: if a subject ends in *s*, its verb does not. There are exceptions, of course. (See more about subject-verb agreement in chapter 2.)

VERB TENSE

Correct verb tense shows when something happens. Let's use *walk* as our sample verb. Here is how this verb differs depending on…

If they're walking right now: They walk.

If they've been walking for some time: They have walked.

If they walked yesterday: They walked.

If they've walked before: They have walked.

If they plan to walk tomorrow: They will walk.

If they will walk until a certain time or for a certain distance: They will have walked.

Like anything else, there are irregular verbs that don't follow these rules.

Practice 2:   Verbs

1   Which verb BEST completes the sentence?

> We _____ an extra day off school next week.

A   have had   C   been having

B   has   D   will have

2   Which sentence uses *break* as a verb?

A   At the break of dawn, the birds began chirping.

B   Hopefully, we can take a lunch break soon.

C   You have to break open the coconut first.

D   Shelly's leg has a break from her fall.

3   Which verb BEST completes the sentence?

> Someone _____ in this creek; they shouldn't fish here anymore.

A   will be fishing   C   fishing

B   has been fishing   D   have been fishing

4   Which verb BEST completes this sentence?

> Bianca _____ as fast as she can tomorrow.

A   has swam   C   is swimming

B   will swim   D   swims

5 **Which sentence uses *stakes* as a verb?**

    A Let's watch as Evan stakes her claim.

    B Hang the flags from the stakes.

    C This race has very high stakes.

    D We don't have enough stakes to raise the tent.

ADJECTIVES

An **adjective** describes a noun. Words like *fierce*, *huge*, and *delicious* are adjectives. An adjective usually comes right before the noun it describes.

    Example: Sean is adding <u>yellow</u> paint to his <u>green</u> artwork.

Some words that are adjectives can also be nouns. For example, *quiet* can be a noun (*I like the quiet*) or an adjective (*This is a quiet night*).

ADVERBS

An **adverb** describes a verb, an adjective, or another adverb. Words like *happily*, *very*, and *often* are adverbs.

Many adverbs look like adjectives. If a descriptive word ends in *-ly*, it may be an adverb. For example, *slow* is usually an adjective. In the sentence *The bus was <u>slow</u>*, the word *slow* describes *bus*. But in the sentence *The bus rolled <u>very slowly</u>*, we can see that *very* describes *slowly* and *slowly* describes *rolled*.

    Example: Sean is <u>eagerly</u> working on his painting.

There are exceptions, of course. *Friendly*, for example, is usually an adjective.

Practice 3: Adjectives and Adverbs

1 **What part of speech is the underlined word in the sentence?**

> The bank robber thought he had a <u>foolproof</u> plan.

    A adjective   C noun

    B adverb   D pronoun

2 **Which sentence uses *green* as an adjective?**

    A The meeting will be held in the village green.

    B It's important to eat greens every day.

    C Tiger Woods reached the green in two strokes.

    D The environmental club created a green plan.

3   Which adverb BEST completes the sentence?

> _____, I didn't make it to the party in time.

A   Unfortunately

B   Unfortunate

C   Unfortune

D   Unfortuney

4   Which sentence uses *well* as an adverb?

A   I hope the meeting went well.

B   Well, it's time to go home.

C   It would be easier to find water if we dug a well.

D   Carolyn watched her sister's eyes well up with tears.

5   Which adjective BEST completes the sentence?

> The car slid sideways down the _____ street.

A   sticky

B   wet

C   black

D   paved

PREPOSITIONS

A **preposition** shows how an item relates to other parts of a sentence.

> **Example:**   Dad's raincoat is <u>inside</u> the car.

> **Example:**   Jumping <u>off</u> the cliff <u>into</u> the lake was so exciting!

Here's a list of common prepositions:

about	behind	except	on	to
above	below	for	onto	toward
across	beneath	from	out	under
after	beside	in	outside	underneath
against	between	inside	over	until
along	beyond	into	past	up
among	by	like	since	upon
around	despite	near	through	with
at	down	of	throughout	within
before	during	off	till	without

Do you see any words in the preposition list that can also be other parts of speech? *Like* can be a verb, and so can *till*. Are there any others?

CONJUNCTIONS

A **conjunction** joins together similar words or phrases. The most common conjunctions are *for, and, nor, but, or, yet,* and *so*. Some people remember these by thinking of the acronym *FANBOYS*.

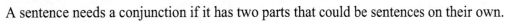

A list of more than one item needs a conjunction.

More than one noun: We have grapes, apples, <u>and</u> bananas. We don't have oranges <u>or</u> tomatoes.

More than one verb: Jordan runs <u>and</u> jumps. Angelica dives <u>and</u> swims.

A sentence needs a conjunction if it has two parts that could be sentences on their own.

Example: Jordan runs, <u>but</u> Angelica swims.

Why does this need a conjunction? "Jordan runs" could be a sentence on its own. So could "Angelica swims." This means the two can be combined with a conjunction.

INTERJECTIONS

An **interjection** expresses emotion without any grammatical connection.

Example: <u>Hey</u>! Bring back that bike.
<u>Ow</u>, I stubbed my toe.
Alberto just stole second base. <u>Yes</u>!

Practice 4: Prepositions, Conjunctions, and Interjections

1 What part of speech is the underlined word in the sentence?

> I think I just saw a cardinal <u>out</u> the window.

A   interjection

B   adjective

C   preposition

D   conjunction

2   Which sentence uses <u>inside</u> as a preposition?

A   The note to your mom is inside the blue folder.

B   Ronny, not so loud; use your inside voice.

C   Giving to charity makes me feel good on the inside.

D   The fastest drivers follow the inside edge.

3   What part of speech is the underlined word in the sentence?

> We can't start the movie yet, <u>but</u> we can have snacks.

A   conjunction

B   verb

C   preposition

D   interjection

4   What part of speech is the underlined word in the sentence?

> <u>Down</u>! Get off the counter, Charlie. Bad dog!

A   preposition

B   conjunction

C   interjection

D   noun

5   Which sentence uses <u>for</u> as a conjunction?

A   De'Angelo mowed lawns for the senior citizens on his street.

B   Can you find something for me to drink?

C   For many kinds of owls, night is the time to be awake.

D   Not all deserts are hot, for many deserts are in colder areas.

CHAPTER 1 SUMMARY

A **noun** is a person, place, or thing.

A **pronoun** stands in for a noun.

A **verb** shows what a person, place, or thing is doing.

An **adjective** describes a noun.

An **adverb** describes a verb, an adjective, or another adverb.

A **preposition** shows how an item relates to other parts of a sentence.

A **conjunction** joins together similar words or phrases.

An **interjection** expresses emotion without any grammatical connection.

CHAPTER 1 REVIEW

1 What part of speech is the underlined word in the sentence?

> The crowd couldn't wait to see what happened <u>next</u>.

A adverb   C preposition

B adjective   D conjunction

2 Which verb BEST completes the sentence?

> The sun _____ out tomorrow.

A came   C will come

B coming   D has come

3 Which sentence uses a pronoun?

A The frightened animal ran back to its nest.

B Listening to music, Luna fell asleep.

C Harris and Nate arm-wrestled for the last piece of pizza.

D Jacoby was wrong to say panda bears aren't bears.

4 What part of speech is the underlined word in the sentence?

> It's clearly not Friday, <u>nor</u> is it three o'clock.

A adverb   B preposition   C conjunction   D verb

5 Which sentence uses *police* as a verb?

A The police officer was fired for breaking the law.

B Sergeant Andrews, carefully police the area.

C Police! I've been robbed!

D Can you give me directions to the police department?

6 What part of speech is the underlined word in the sentence?

> Her companion was a <u>retired</u> banker named Marty Stone.

A conjunction   B adverb   C verb   D adjective

7 Which sentence uses *good* as a noun?

A The president claimed to care about the good of the people.

B I wasn't having a good time camping in the woods.

C It's a good thing we didn't both wear the same sweater tonight.

D Good! Now maybe you've learned your lesson.

8 What part of speech is the underlined word in the sentence?

> The kids <u>usually</u> launched their boats near the bridge.

A preposition   C adjective

B adverb   D pronoun

9 Which sentence uses *run* as an interjection?

A The one-mile run will be at noon.

B Run! The stampede is heading this way.

C Mika was surprised at how fast she could run.

D Run down the menu, and see what you want to eat.

10 What part of speech is the underlined word in this sentence?

> The young mare <u>galloped</u> around the coral while the cowboy tried to lasso it.

A preposition   C verb

B adjective   D noun

Chapter 2
Usage and Grammar

This chapter covers the following GPS-based CRCT standard:

ELA5C1 The student demonstrates understanding and control of the rules of the English language, realizing that usage involves the appropriate application of conventions and grammar in both written and spoken formats. The student	
c. Uses and identifies verb phrases and verb tenses.	**g.** Uses additional knowledge of correct mechanics ... and correct Standard English ... when writing, revising, and editing.

How do you tell others what you want, need, or think? Usually, you speak or write to send your message. Whether speaking or writing, you want others to understand what you are saying. Using words correctly is an important way to help others understand you.

VERBS

A **verb** describes an action. *Swim, leap, dribble, sleep,* and *scream* are all verbs.

A **verb phrase** is the verb plus the complement. (A complement is the part of a sentence that comes after the verb and makes the sentence complete.)

Example: He <u>wrote the math problem on the white board</u>.

The underlined part is the verb phrase. It contains the verb *wrote* plus the complement, "the math problem on the white board."

VERB TENSE

Verb tense tells when the action was done or will be done. The three basic tenses are past (already done), present (being done now), and future (to be done later).

Verbs Tenses		
Tense	**Description**	**Example**
Past	action that has happened	He <u>batted</u> in the last inning.
Simple present	action that is about to happen or happens all the time	Santo <u>bats</u> now. He always <u>bats</u> before Jeremy.
Present progressive	action in progress	Kyle <u>is batting</u>. Watch!
Future	action in the future	Omar <u>will bat</u> after Billy.

When using verbs, it is important to use the correct tense.

   Incorrect: Tomorrow, Kaya painted a picture.

   Correct: Tomorrow, Kaya will paint a picture.

When you are choosing a tense to write in, stick with it. If you are writing about an event that happened in the past, the verbs you use should be in the past tense.

REGULAR AND IRREGULAR VERBS

Most verbs are regular. This means they follow certain rules when they change tense. Irregular verbs do not follow these rules. You will need to learn which verbs are regular and which are not.

To make the past tense of a regular verb, add *ed* to the end.

   Example: *concern + ed = concerned*

An irregular verb changes spelling in the past tense.

   Example: *See* does not become *seed*. It becomes *saw*.

The main place we see a verb's irregularity is in the past tense. The next table shows some irregular verbs and how they form the past tense.

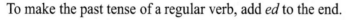

Irregular Verbs			
Present Tense		**Past Tense**	
fly	feel	flew	felt
do	catch	did	caught
take		took	

SUBJECT-VERB AGREEMENT

The subject of a sentence is who or what is doing the action. As you already know, the verb describes the action. To make sense, a sentence must have **subject-verb agreement**.

Subjects and verbs must agree. This means that if the subject is singular, the verb must be singular. If the subject is plural, the verb must be plural. Singular means "one." Plural means "more than one."

Singular subject and verb: The pie is done.

Plural subject and verb: The cookies are done.

The first thing to do is identify the subject and the verb. Next, make sure the verb matches the subject so that they are both singular or both plural. If they do not match, correct them. Here are some examples of singular and plural subjects and verbs.

Example:

The *runner is* nearing the finish line.
The *runners are* nearing the finish line.
She goes to the city on the weekend.
The *sisters go* to the city on the weekend.
He likes to play video games.
They like to play video games.

MORE THAN ONE SUBJECT

Some sentences have **more than one subject**. Here is how to handle these sentences.

When both subjects are singular and connected by *or* or *nor*, use a singular verb.

Example: My brother or my sister makes dinner on Saturdays.
                          subj.   subj.   verb

When singular subjects are joined by *and*, use a plural verb.

Example: A baby and a toddler are both young children.
                   subj.   subj.   verb

PRONOUNS AS SUBJECTS

Pronouns can be subjects too. They can be singular or plural. Here are some common singular and plural pronouns.

Singular pronouns: *he, it, she, I, my*

Plural pronouns: *we, they, their*

Some pronouns sound plural but are actually singular. The following pronouns are singular. They need singular verbs.

everyone, each, anybody, someone, everybody, anyone, neither, nobody

Example: <u>Each</u> of the horses <u>runs</u> fast.

Some pronouns can be followed by words that people mistake for the subject of the sentence. Don't be confused by "the horses." This is not the subject. *Each* is the subject.

Practice 1: Verbs

For each of sentence, choose the verb that BEST completes the sentence.

1   Because the pool was closed, we _____ on the playground instead.

A   is playing   C   play

B   played   D   playing

2   Next year, Jon ____ lunch at school.

A   will eat   C   eating

B   did eat   D   ate

3   The ringmaster _____ the next act.

A   is announces

B   are announcing

C   is announcing

D   are announces

4   Which sentence uses the correct verb form?

A   An apple and a pear is lying on the table.

B   An apple and a pear are lying on the table.

C   An apple and a pear lyings on the table.

D   An apple and a pear lying on the table.

5   Which sentence uses the correct verb form?

A   Chocolate cake or cherry pie are my favorite dessert.

B   Chocolate cake or cherry pie is being my favorite dessert.

C   Chocolate cake or cherry pie were my favorite dessert.

D   Chocolate cake or cherry pie is my favorite dessert.

6   Which sentence uses the correct verb form?

A   Each of the swimmers were given a medal.

B   Each of the swimmers was gave a medal.

C   Each of the swimmers was given a medal.

D   Each of the swimmers were gave a medal.

STANDARD ENGLISH

Part of being understood is using words correctly. This is called using **standard English**. Here are some common grammar errors that do not use standard English.

DOUBLE NEGATIVES

A **double negative** is the use of two negatives in a single sentence.

Here are some words that are considered negative.

no, nobody, none, hardly, nothing, nowhere

When you combine negative words, you create a double negative.

> **Example:** "I <u>don't</u> want <u>none</u> of those pencils."

This sentence actually means "I want some of those pencils."
The two negatives cancel each other out, making a positive. A double negative is not standard English and needs to be corrected. To correct this sentence, you could write it like this:

> "I don't want any of those pencils."

SPLIT INFINITIVES

As you read earlier in the chapter, a verb can be more than one word.

> **Example:** Would you be excited <u>to win</u> the class spelling bee?

To win is the complete verb. This is called the infinitive form of the verb. *To sing, to dive, to work*, and *to worry* are some more examples of the infinitive form. Do not separate these parts of a verb. If you do, this is a **split infinitive**, which is incorrect.

> **Incorrect:** The team was afraid <u>to</u> badly <u>lose</u> to its opponent.

> **Correct:** The team was afraid <u>to lose</u> badly to its opponent.

MISPLACED MODIFIERS

A **modifier** is a word or phrase that describes something. Put the modifier as close as possible to what it is describing. A **misplaced modifier** makes the meaning less clear.

> **Incorrect:** The lady was walking the dog in the wig.

Was the dog wearing a wig? Probably not!

> **Correct:** The lady in the wig was walking the dog.

PRONOUN-ANTECEDENT AGREEMENT

You read about pronouns in chapter 1. Just as subjects and verbs agree, so do pronouns and the words they replace. The words that pronouns replace are called antecedents. If an antecedent is singular, the pronoun that goes with it must be singular. If an antecedent is plural, the pronoun that goes with it must be plural. This is called **pronoun-antecedent agreement**. Remember that some pronouns sound plural but are actually singular.

Singular pronoun and antecedent:

The <u>dog</u> pulled at <u>its</u> chain.

   antecedent   pronoun

Plural pronoun and antecedent:

<u>Students</u> should leave <u>their</u> backpacks in the hall.

antecedent   pronoun

Practice 2: Nonstandard English

Which sentence in each set uses standard English?

1   A I don't want no potatoes with my dinner.

     (B) I don't want any potatoes with my dinner.

     C I don't not want potatoes with my dinner.

     D I am not wanting no potatoes with my dinner.

2   A The dance instructor said that to slowly twirl is the right way.

     (B) The dance instructor said that to slowly be twirling is the right way.

     C The dance instructor said that to quickly twirl is the right way.

     D The dance instructor said that to twirl slowly is the right way.

3   A The baker high on the shelf put the cake.

     (B) The baker put the cake high on the shelf.

     C The baker high on the shelf had put the cake.

     D The baker on the high shelf put the cake.

4 (A) The girls sang her part one more time.

     B The girls sang they part one more time.

     C The girls sang them part one more time.

     D The girls sang their part one more time.

5 A   That boy's shoe just came off of their foot.

B   That boy's shoe just came off of they foot.

C   That boy's shoe just came off of her foot.

(D) That boy's shoe just came off of his foot.

CHAPTER 2 SUMMARY

Verbs show action. **Subjects and verbs must agree**. When a verb has more than one subject, look for *or* and *and* to decide if the verb should be singular or plural.

Verb tense tells when the action is done. **Irregular verbs** do not follow standard rules when they change tense.

Nonstandard English needs correction. Avoid **double negatives**; they cancel each other out. Keep the two parts of an **infinitive** together. Put the **modifier** as close to what it is describing as possible so your meaning is clear.

Pronouns and antecedents must agree.

CHAPTER 2 REVIEW

Which sentence in each set uses correct English?

1 A   I can't hardly see the movie screen from this seat.

(B) I can't barely see the movie screen from this seat.

C   I cannot hardly see the movie screen from this seat.

D   I can hardly see the movie screen from this seat.

2 A   Last night, Zach ate dinner, brushed his teeth, and was going to bed.

B   Last night, Zach ate dinner, brushed his teeth, and goed to bed.

(C) Last night, Zach ate dinner, brushed his teeth, and went to bed.

D   Last night, Zach eats dinner, brushes his teeth, and was going to bed.

3 A   Maya decided to slowly walk into the kitchen with the stack of plates.

(B) Maya decided to walk slowly into the kitchen with the stack of plates.

C   Maya decided to walk into the slowly kitchen with the stack of plates.

D   Maya decided to slow walk into the kitchen with the stack of plates.

4 A Anybody are welcome at the party.

   B Anybody welcome at the party.

   C Anybody is welcome at the party.

   D Anybody welcome is at the party.

5 A Peanuts and fish is a duck's favorite foods.

   B Peanuts and fish be a duck's favorite foods.

   C Peanuts and fish are being a duck's favorite foods.

   D Peanuts and fish are a duck's favorite foods.

6 A When a runner wins a race, he celebrates.

   B When a runner wins a race, he celebrate.

   C When a runner wins a race, he is celebrates.

   D When a runner wins a race, he is celebrate.

7 A The clowns changed his costumes before the last act.

   B The clowns changed they costumes before the last act.

   C The clowns changed their costumes before the last act.

   D The clowns will changed their costumes before the last act.

8 A The blue sweater or the green sweater are the one I am going to pick.

   B The blue sweater or the green sweater is the one I am going to pick.

   C The blue sweater or the green sweater the one I am going to pick.

   D The blue sweaters or the green sweaters is the one I am going to pick.

CRCT

5

5th GRADE

Chapter 3
Punctuation

This chapter covers the following GPS-based CRCT standard:

ELA5C1 The student demonstrates understanding and control of the rules of the English language, realizing that usage involves the appropriate application of conventions and grammar in both written and spoken formats. The student	
f. Uses and identifies correct mechanics (e.g., apostrophes, quotation marks, comma use in compound sentences, paragraph indentations) and correct sentence structure (e.g., elimination of sentence fragments and run-ons).	g. Uses additional knowledge of correct mechanics (e.g., apostrophes, quotation marks, comma use in compound sentences, paragraph indentations), correct sentence structure (e.g., elimination of fragments and run-ons), and correct Standard English spelling (e.g., commonly used homophones) when writing, revising, and editing.

Every sentence uses **punctuation**. Punctuation helps the reader understand the sentence. There are a few basic kinds of punctuation.

END MARKS

End marks do exactly what they sound like they do; they mark the end of sentences. Every sentence needs one end mark. These are the three end marks: periods, question marks, and exclamation marks.

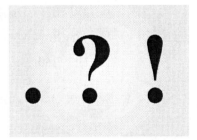

A **period** ends a sentence that declares something. That means the sentence simply makes a statement. This is called a declarative sentence. Periods also are used to end imperative sentences, which give directions or orders. Periods are the most common end marks.

> **Examples:** Lions originated in Africa.
>
> It's really hot outside today.
>
> Open your book to page fifty-eight.
>
> Take off that hat.

A **question mark** ends a sentence that asks a question. Questions are called interrogative sentences.

Examples: How long does the average lion live?

Was it hot at the beach yesterday?

An **exclamation mark** ends a sentence that expresses intense emotion. This kind of sentence is called an exclamatory sentence.

Examples: Help! The lion escaped!

It's so hot the ice sculpture melted!

Practice 1: End Marks

1 What type of sentence is this?

Ashley wants to stay home.

A declarative   C exclamatory

B imperative   D interrogative

2   Which end mark should end this sentence?

Why does Grandpa like to keep so much old stuff

A period   C question mark

B comma   D exclamation mark

3   Which sentence should end in an exclamation mark?

A Nick is learning how to change a tire

B When are we going to visit St. Louis

C The fireworks last night were amazing

D Has Bethany ever done a backflip

4   Which end mark should end this sentence?

You have gotten much better at math this year

A exclamation mark

B period

C quotation mark

D question mark

5 What type of sentence is this?

Open the window to let in some air.

A exclamatory

B declarative

C interrogative

D imperative

COMMAS

Commas separate parts of sentences.

Commas separate items in lists of three or more.

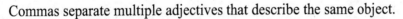

Example: Don't forget your shoes, coat, belt, and purse.

Some people follow different rules on whether to use the final comma in a list or not. Ask your teacher whether or not you should use the final comma before a conjunction.

Commas separate multiple adjectives that describe the same object.

Example: The big, red house is being painted blue.

Commas separate extra information from the rest of the sentence.

Example: My sister, who works as a doctor, has tickets to the show.

Commas separate the names of cities, states, and countries.

Example: We flew from Atlanta, Georgia, to Nuremberg, Germany.

Commas separate parts of dates.

When a day and month are used with a year, a comma separates the date and year (as in *January 31, 2010*).

When a day of the week is added to a date, a comma separates the day and date (as in *Sunday, January 31, 2010*).

A comma also follows at the end of the date.

When only a month is used with a year, no commas are needed (as in *January 2010*).

Examples: On Monday, May 17, 2008, we bought a new house.

On May 17, 2008, we bought a new house.

In May 2008 we bought a new house.

Practice 2: Commas

1 Which sentence uses commas correctly?

A My neighbor's big loud dog kept us awake all night.

B My neighbor's big, loud dog kept us awake all night.

C My neighbor's big, loud, dog kept us awake all night.

D My neighbor's big, loud, dog, kept us awake all night.

2 Which sentence uses commas correctly?

A I was born on, Monday December 6, 1999, in Valdosta Georgia.

B I was born on Monday December 6, 1999, in Valdosta, Georgia.

C I was born on Monday, December 6, 1999, in Valdosta, Georgia.

D I was born on, Monday, December 6 1999, in Valdosta Georgia.

3 Which sentence uses commas correctly?

A Please take this box, which is full of tools to the back yard.

B Please take this box which is full of tools, to the back yard.

C Please take this box which is full of tools to the back yard.

D Please take this box, which is full of tools, to the back yard.

4 Which sentence uses commas correctly?

A Rasheeda is helping her mom move the dresser, desk, and table.

B Rasheeda is helping her mom move the dresser desk, and table.

C Rasheeda is helping her mom move the, dresser, desk, and table.

D Rasheeda is helping her mom move the dresser desk and table.

5 Which sentence uses commas correctly?

A Does a space shuttle go fast, enough to break the sound barrier?

B Does a space shuttle go, fast enough to break the sound barrier?

C Does a space shuttle go fast enough, to break the sound barrier?

D Does a space shuttle go fast enough to break the sound barrier?

QUOTATION MARKS

Pairs of **quotation marks** show where a quotation begins and ends. A quotation is a statement made by someone besides the author.

Example: I was going to keep running until I heard Deshaun say, "Stop!"

COLONS

Colons are mostly used to introduce lists.

Example: The honorees came from the following countries: Sudan, Uganda, and Nigeria.

In this sentence, *Sudan, Uganda, and Nigeria* is the list. The colon separates the list from the rest of the sentence.

If the part of the sentence that comes before the list is a complete thought, then the list needs a colon. Not all lists begin with colons. For example, look at these sentences.

The honorees came from countries like Sudan, Uganda, and Nigeria.

As you can see, "The honorees came from countries like" is not a complete thought. This means no colon is necessary, as the list is a critical part of the sentence.

APOSTROPHES

Apostrophes are used in two ways.

An apostrophe shows when a word is a contraction. A contraction is a pair of words (like *do not*) shortened into one word (like *don't*).

Example: Couldn't you let Nick go with you, since he won't get to go later?

Couldn't is short for *could not*. And *won't* is short for *will not*. The apostrophes show which words are contractions.

An apostrophe is part of the possessive form of nouns.

Example: Izzy's teeth hurt after eating all of Katie's candy.

In this example, the teeth belong to Izzy; therefore, they are Izzy's teeth. An apostrophe and *s* show possession. The same is true for Katie's candy.

Practice 3:   Quotation Marks, Colons, and Apostrophes

1 Which sentence uses quotation marks correctly?

A   An eye for an eye only ends up making the whole world blind, said Gandhi.

B   "An eye for an eye only ends up making the whole world blind," said Gandhi.

C   "An eye for an eye only ends up making the whole world blind, said Gandhi."

D   "An eye for an eye only ends up making the whole world blind, said Gandhi.

2   Which sentence uses apostrophes correctly?

A   You shouldn't break other people's things.

B   You shouldnt break other people's things.

C   You shouldn't break other peoples things.

D   You shouldn't break other peoples thing's.

3   Which sentence uses quotation marks correctly?

A   Hey Emily, Austin asked, is the movie over yet?

B   "Hey Emily, Austin asked, is the movie over yet?"

C   Hey Emily, "Austin asked," is the movie over yet?

D   "Hey Emily," Austin asked, "is the movie over yet?"

4   Which sentence uses apostrophes correctly?

A   We'll always remember our trips to Grandmas house.

B   We'll always remember our trips to Grandma's house.

C   Wel'l always remember our trips to Grandma's house.

D   We'll always remember our trip's to Grandma's house.

5   Which sentence uses colons correctly?

A   Tell me about: your favorite music, TV shows, and movies.

B   Tell me about your favorite: music, TV shows, and movies.

C   Tell me about your favorite entertainment: music, TV shows, and movies.

D   Tell me about: your favorite entertainment music, TV shows, and movies.

6   Which sentence uses quotation marks correctly?

A   "How long does it take to become a good photographer? asked Trey.

B   "How long does it take to become a good photographer? asked Trey."

C   "How long does it take to become a good photographer?" asked Trey.

D   "How long does it take to become a good photographer? asked" Trey.

SENTENCE TYPES

In the last section, we looked at how commas separate words. Commas also separate larger parts of **sentences**.

COMPOUND SENTENCES

An independent clause is a group of words that can stand on its own as a complete thought. A **compound sentence** is made of two independent clauses. These two parts are usually connected by a conjunction (*for, and, nor, but, or, yet, so*) and a comma.

> **Example:** Just do your best, and don't worry about what the judges think.

"Just do your best" is an independent clause. "Don't worry about what the judges think" is also an independent clause. They're properly separated by a comma and the conjunction *and*.

COMPLEX SENTENCES

A **complex sentence** is a independent clause plus a dependent clause. A dependent clause is a group of words that cannot stand on its own as a complete thought.

> **Example 1:** I ate the meal that you cooked.

In this example, "I ate the meal" is a independent clause. "That you cooked" is a dependent clause. If a comma were added between the two ("I ate the meal, that you cooked"), the sentence would not make sense.

> **Example 2:** When you cooked the meal, I ate it.

In this example, "I ate it" is a independent clause. "When you cooked the meal" is not. For clarity, this sentence needs a comma to separate its two parts.

COMPOUND-COMPLEX SENTENCES

A **compound-complex sentence** has multiple independent clauses and at least one dependent clause.

> **Example 1:** The messy dog lived in the backyard, but the cat, who didn't make messes, lived inside the house.

The messy dog lived in the backyard is an independent clause. So is *The cat lived inside the house*. Combining the two requires a comma and a *but*. Adding the dependent clause *who didn't make messes*, which describes *cat*, requires another pair of commas.

> **Example 2:** Before going home, Carly started washing the dishes, but Derrick, hoping to impress her, insisted on finishing them.

Here, "Carly started washing the dishes" and "Derrick insisted on finishing them" are independent clauses. *Before going home* and *hoping to impress her* are the dependent clauses.

Practice 4: Sentence Types

1 Which sentence uses commas correctly?

A The most recent ice age began about twelve thousand years ago lasting about one thousand years.

B The most recent ice age began about twelve thousand years ago, lasting about one thousand years.

C The most recent ice age, began about twelve thousand years ago, lasting about one thousand years.

D The most recent ice age began, about twelve thousand years ago, lasting about one thousand years.

2 Which sentence uses commas correctly?

A Olympic boxing, which has never allowed women to compete before will do so in 2012.

B Olympic boxing which has never allowed women to compete before, will do so in 2012.

C Olympic boxing, which has never allowed women to compete before, will do so in 2012.

D Olympic boxing which has never allowed women to compete before will do so in, 2012.

3 Which sentence uses a colon correctly?

A We celebrate: the following holidays Christmas, Hanukkah, Kwanzaa, and others.

B We celebrate the following: holidays Christmas, Hanukkah, Kwanzaa, and others.

C We celebrate the following holidays Christmas: Hanukkah, Kwanzaa, and others.

D We celebrate the following holidays: Christmas, Hanukkah, Kwanzaa, and others.

4 Which sentence uses commas correctly?

A I was scared but I didn't run away.

B I was, scared but I didn't run away.

C I was scared, but I didn't run away.

D I was scared, but, I didn't run away.

5 **Which sentence uses commas correctly?**

    A   The dog that you gave me, barked at me and it bit my hand.

    B   The dog that you gave me, barked at me, and it bit my hand.

    C   The dog that you gave me barked at me, and it bit my hand.

    D   The dog, that you gave me, barked at me and it bit my hand.

6 **Which sentence uses commas correctly?**

    A   Melissa invited me to her birthday party, but I had swim practice that night.

    B   Melissa invited me to her birthday party but I had swim practice that night.

    C   Melissa invited me, to her birthday party, but I had swim practice that night.

    D   Melissa invited me to her birthday party but I had swim practice, that night.

CHAPTER 3 SUMMARY

End marks mark the end of sentences. These are the three end marks:

- A **period** ends a sentence that declares something.
- A **question mark** ends a sentence that asks a question.
- An **exclamation mark** ends a sentence that expresses intense emotion.

Commas separate parts of sentences.

Pairs of **quotation marks** show where a quotation begins and ends.

Colons are used to introduce lists.

Apostrophes indicate contraction or show possession.

A **compound sentence** is made of two independent clauses.

A **complex sentence** is a independent clause with an extra part, called a dependent clause.

A **compound-complex sentence** has multiple independent clauses and at least one dependent clause.

CHAPTER 3 REVIEW

1 Which end mark should end this sentence?

> Pandas prefer to eat bamboo even though it doesn't give them very much energy

A exclamation mark

B question mark

C apostrophe

D period

2 What type of sentence is this?

> One scientist wondered if an animal could become a different kind of animal by having its blood changed.

A interrogative

B declarative

C exclamatory

D imperative

3 Which sentence uses commas correctly?

A The world's tallest waterfall, is in Bolivar, Venezuela.

B The world's tallest waterfall is in Bolivar Venezuela.

C The world's tallest waterfall is in, Bolivar, Venezuela.

D The world's tallest waterfall is in Bolivar, Venezuela.

**Angel Falls
Venezuela**

4 Which sentence uses commas correctly?

A Flash floods are usually sudden dangerous, and frightening.

B Flash floods are usually, sudden, dangerous, and frightening.

C Flash floods are usually sudden dangerous and frightening.

D Flash floods are usually sudden, dangerous, and frightening.

5 **Which sentence uses colons correctly?**

   A The menu includes: chicken, pizza, and ice cream.

   B The menu includes chicken, pizza, and ice cream.

   C The menu: includes chicken, pizza, and ice cream.

   D The menu includes chicken: pizza, and ice cream.

6 **Which sentence uses commas correctly?**

   A The Taylor Swift concert in April 2009 was fun.

   B The Taylor Swift concert in April, 2009 was fun.

   C The Taylor Swift concert in April, 2009, was fun.

   D The Taylor Swift concert in, April 2009, was fun.

7 **Which sentence uses commas correctly?**

   A Everyone seemed to think it was a miserable, rainy day, but I had fun.

   B Everyone seemed to think it was a miserable, rainy day but I had fun.

   C Everyone seemed to think it was a miserable, rainy, day, but I had fun.

   D Everyone seemed to think it was a miserable rainy day, but I had fun.

8 **Which sentence uses quotation marks correctly?**

   A If this phone breaks, you can return it for a new one," said the salesman.

   B "If this phone breaks, you can return it for a new one, said the salesman.

   C "If this phone breaks, you can return it for a new one," said the salesman.

   D "If this phone breaks, you can return it for a new one, said the salesman."

9 **Which sentence uses commas correctly?**

   A When Jasmine was thirteen, her family moved to Knoxville, Tennessee.

   B When Jasmine was thirteen, her family moved to, Knoxville, Tennessee.

   C When Jasmine was thirteen, her family moved to Knoxville Tennessee.

   D When Jasmine was thirteen, her family, moved to Knoxville, Tennessee.

10 Which sentence uses apostrophes correctly?

A Maurices friends couldn't explain why they'd shown up so late.

B Maurice's friend's couldn't explain why they'd shown up so late.

C Maurice's friends couldn't explain why theyd shown up so late.

D Maurice's friends couldn't explain why they'd shown up so late.

11 Which sentence uses commas correctly?

A The engineer, who was on his way to the facility, was thinking of ways to solve the problem.

B The engineer who was on his way to the facility, was thinking of ways to solve the problem.

C The engineer, who was on his way to the facility was thinking of ways to solve the problem.

D The engineer, who was on his way to the facility, was thinking, of ways to solve the problem.

12 Which sentence uses colons correctly?

A My cousin is trying to choose between these colleges Auburn, Clemson, and Florida State.

B My cousin is trying to choose: between these colleges Auburn, Clemson, and Florida State.

C My cousin is trying to choose between: these colleges Auburn, Clemson, and Florida State.

D My cousin is trying to choose between these colleges: Auburn, Clemson, and Florida State.

ENGLISH LANGUAGE ARTS

CRCT

5

5th GRADE

Chapter 4
Spelling

This chapter covers the following GPS-based CRCT standard:

ELA5C1 The student demonstrates understanding and control of the rules of the English language, realizing that usage involves the appropriate application of conventions and grammar in both written and spoken formats. The student

g. Uses additional knowledge of ... correct Standard English spelling (e.g., commonly used homophones) when writing, revising, and editing.

In chapter 2, you read how using words correctly helps others to understand what you are trying to say. Using correct **spelling** is another way you can make your writing easier to understand. Spelling helps make your meaning clear. Misspellings can be confusing to your reader.

LEARNING CORRECT SPELLINGS

The best way to **learn how to spell words** is to read as much as you can. When you read, you see many words in context. You learn how they are used and see how they are spelled. You can also work crossword puzzles and other word games. These help you use find and use words with their correct spellings.

You probably have learned new words every week in school. A good way to improve spelling is to keep a list of words you do not know well. Look them up in the dictionary. Practice using them when you write.

SPELLING RULES

There are many **spelling rules**. You have learned these rules in school. You can find them in language arts books, writing books, and style books. Here are just a few rules to keep in mind.

SPELLING PLURAL NOUNS

Most words follow some common rules of spelling. Here are some of the most common spelling rules for **making words plural**.

Rule 1.   **Make most words plural by adding *s*.**

hawk + s = hawks

president + s = presidents

Rule 2.   **If a noun ends with *ch*, *sh*, *s*, *ss*, or *x*, add *es* to form the plural.**

watch + es = watches

compass + es = compasses

Rule 3.   **For words that end with *y* and have a consonant before the *y*, change the *y* to *i* before adding the *es* ending.**

factory + es = factories

berry + es = berries

Rule 4.   **Some nouns take a completely different spelling when going from singular to plural. Or, they may not change at all! Memorize irregular words like these.**

Irregular Plurals	
Singular	**Plural**
deer	deer
mouse	mice
woman	women

SPELLING VERB TENSES

Most verbs follow some common rules of spelling when they change tense. Study these to help you remember how to **spell verb tenses**. Here are some common spelling rules for verbs ending with *ing*.

Rule 1.   **For most verbs, simply add *ing* to the end of a word.**

visit + ing = visiting

tunnel + ing = tunneling

Rule 2. When a word ends with a silent *e*, drop the *e* before adding *ing*.

decide + ing = deciding

imagine + ing = imagining

Rule 3. When a word ends in a *y*, do not drop the *y* before adding *ing*.

study + ing = studying

try + ing = trying

Rule 4. If the word has one syllable and ends with a single consonant, double the consonant before adding *ing*.

trim + ing = trimming

swim + ing = swimming

Rule 5. For words with two syllables, look at which syllable is stressed. If it is the first, do not double the consonant. If the second syllable is stressed, double the consonant. You will need to learn these words.

Stress on first syllable:

tunnel + ing = tunneling

visit + ing = visiting

Stress on second syllable:

begin + ing = beginning

refer + ing = referring

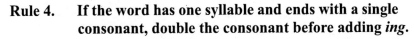

Practice 1: Spelling Rules

Choose the correct spelling for each underlined word.

1 How many <u>wifes</u> did Henry VIII have?

    A wives   C wifs

    B wifess   D wiffes

2 The truck brought <u>supplys</u> to the Army camp.

    A suppliees   C supplliyes

    B supplyes   D supplies

3 Watch how the spider is <u>attachhing</u> its web to the ceiling.

    A attachying   C attaching

    B atacheing   D atachying

4 There is a blizzard, so expect <u>delayes</u> at the airport.

A delaies   C delayies

B delays   D delais

5 We are <u>chooseing</u> from a list of three topics for our report.

A chooseng   C choossing

B choosing   D chosing

6 Watch out! You're <u>spiling</u> your milk!

A spilling   C spiliying

B spilying   D spliting

HOMOPHONES

Homophones are words that sound alike but have different meanings and different spellings. It is important to use the correct spelling of these words so readers can understand your writing.

Here are some examples of homophones.

Common Homophones	
sea, see	bored, board
missed, mist	male, mail
ring, wring	here, hear
your, you're	past, passed

It is just as important to use the correct homophone as it is to spell other words correctly. Memorize the meanings of homophones. This is the best way to remember which is which.

Practice 2: Homophones

Choose the correct homophone for each sentence. Use a dictionary if you need help deciding the correct answer.

1 When is your book _____ back at the library?

A do   C dew

B due   D doo

2 _____ soccer cleats are lying on the floor?

A Whoos   C Whos

B Who's   D Whose

3 Are _____ allowed to talk in the halls?

   A whe

   B we

   C wee

   D wii

4 **Fashion models sometimes _____ some strange-looking clothes.**

   A were

   B where

   C wear

   D wheer

5 **The rebels will soon _____ power from the king.**

   A seas   C seize

   B sees   D seeze

Activity: Homophones

For each of the words below, write a sentence that shows the word's meaning. The first one is done for you.

<u>bare</u> After we cleared the dishes, the table was bare.

<u>bear</u> The hikers saw a bear in the woods and ran away as fast as they could.

one _____

won _____

bow _____

bough _____

brake _____

break _____

it's _____

its _____

CHAPTER 4 SUMMARY

When you write, correct **spelling** makes your meaning clear.

Learn correct spelling by reading, working word games, and using the dictionary.

Follow common **spelling rules**, like adding *s* or *es* to the end of most words. Memorize irregular spellings.

Memorize the correct spelling of **homophones**, which are words that sound alike.

CHAPTER 4 REVIEW

Choose the spelling correction to make in each sentence.

1   **Have you heard that gooses fly in a triangle formation?**

   A   Change *heard* to *heerd*.

   B   Change *heard* to *herd*.

   C   Change *gooses* to *geese*.

   D   Change *gooses* to *gooss*.

2   **My dog always burys her bones under the porch.**

   A   Change *burys* to *buries*.

   B   Change *bones* to *boness*.

   C   Change *burys* to *bures*.

   D   Change *bones* to *bons*.

3   **Volunteers often help during searchs for lost children.**

   A   Change *volunteers* to *volunteeres*.

   B   Change *children* to *childs*.

   C   Change *volunteers* to *volunteeres*.

   D   Change *searchs* to *searches*.

4   I wonder if their going to vote in the election.

A   Change *their* to *they're*.

B   Change *their* to *there*.

C   Change *election* to *electione*.

D   Change *going* to *goeing*.

5   My cousin tossed the ball threw the window.

A   Change *cousin* to *cousins*.

B   Change *threw* to *through*.

C   Change *threw* to *throw*.

D   Change *cousin* to *counsines*.

6   In some areas of the country, leafs do not change color in the fall.

A   Change *leafs* to *leafes*.

B   Change *areas* to *areaes*.

C   Change *change* to *changing*.

D   Change *leafs* to *leaves*.

7   Pirates are famous for stealing and buryying treasures.

A   Change *treasures* to *treasurees*.

B   Change *pirates* to *piratees*.

C   Change *pirates* to *pirats*.

D   Change *buryying* to *burying*.

8   Did you just hear someone breatheing?

A   Change *hear* to *here*.

B   Change *breatheing* to *breathing*.

C   Change *hear* to *heer*.

D   Change *breatheing* to *breathhing*.

9 **He is behind the barn spliting wood.**

A Change *wood* to *would*.

B Change *wood* to *woould*.

C Change *spliting* to *splitting*.

D Change *spliting* to *spliteing*.

10 **Rita says she likes swimming better then bicycling.**

A Change *says* to *sez*.

B Change *swimming* to *swiming*.

C Change *then* to *than*.

D Change *bicycling* to *bycicling*.

CRCT

5

5th GRADE

Chapter 5
Working with Sentences

This chapter covers the following GPS-based CRCT standard:

ELA5C1 The student demonstrates understanding and control of the rules of the English language, realizing that usage involves the appropriate application of conventions and grammar in both written and spoken formats. The student	
b. Expands or reduces sentences (e.g., adding or deleting modifiers, combining or revising sentences).	**e.** Varies the sentence structure by kind (declarative, interrogative, imperative, and exclamatory sentences and functional fragments), order, and complexity (simple, compound, complex, and compound-complex).
f. Uses and identifies correct mechanics (e.g., apostrophes, quotation marks, comma use in compound sentences, paragraph indentations) and correct sentence structure (e.g., elimination of sentence fragments and run-ons).	**g.** Uses additional knowledge of … correct sentence structure … when writing, revising, and editing.

SENTENCE STRUCTURE

A **sentence** is a complete thought. There are different kinds of sentences. One component of good writing is variety. Use different kinds of sentences to add variety to your writing.

SIMPLE SENTENCES

A **simple sentence** is also called an independent clause. An **independent clause** can stand alone as its own sentence. It has a subject and a predicate. A predicate is made up of at least a verb. Sometimes it also has an object, modifier, or other elements.

> **Example:** She sang.

She is the subject, and *sang* is the predicate (verb).

> **Example:** I want an iPod for my birthday.

I is the subject, and *want an iPod for my birthday* is the predicate (verb + object + prepositional phrase).

COMPOUND SENTENCES

A **compound sentence** is two independent clauses joined by a coordinating conjunction.

Coordinating Conjunctions		
and	or	for
but	nor	yet
		so

Put a comma before the coordinating conjunction in a compound sentence.

> **Example:** Jen prefers knee socks, but Jamie prefers no socks.

"Jen prefers knee socks" can stand alone as a sentence. "Jamie prefers no socks" can stand alone as a sentence. The coordinating conjunction is *but*. Notice the comma before *but*.

COMPLEX SENTENCES

A **complex sentence** is an independent clause plus one or more dependent clauses. A **dependent clause** cannot stand alone as a sentence.

> **Example:** After we finish our homework, we are allowed to play outside.

"After we finish our homework" cannot stand alone as its own sentence. It is the dependent clause. "We are allowed to play outside" can stand alone as a sentence. It is the independent clause.

Dependent clauses start with words like these:

- if
- after
- unless
- when
- since
- before
- though
- because
- while
- although

If the dependent clause comes first, separate the two clauses with a comma. If the independent clause comes first, do not use a comma.

> **Example:** Although we all like pasta, Jorge's favorite food is pizza.

"Although we all like pasta" is a dependent clause. It comes first, so the two are separated by a comma.

We all like pasta although Jorge's favorite food is pizza.

"We all like pasta" is an independent clause. It comes first, so there is no comma.

COMPOUND-COMPLEX SENTENCES

A **compound-complex sentence** has at least two independent clauses and at least one dependent clause.

> **Example:** While we waited for our food, three other diners were served, and no new customers came in.

"While we waited for our food" is a dependent clause. "Three other diners were served" is an independent clause. "No new customers came in" is an independent clause.

Practice 1: Sentence Structures

What sentence structure does each sentence use?

1 **Without wings, it is unlikely that we will ever fly.**

    A simple

    B compound

    C complex

    D compound-complex

2 **You should take off your muddy shoes before you track mud into the house.**

    A simple   C complex

    B compound   D compound-complex

3 **Kenzie is taking violin this year, and Will is playing soccer.**

    A simple   C complex

    B compound   D compound-complex

4 **After you take the cookies from the oven, let them sit for ten minutes, but move them to a plate as soon as they are cool.**

    A simple   C complex

    B compound   D compound-complex

5 **Dad says we should take out the trash right away.**

    A simple   C complex

    B compound   D compound-complex

6 **I like going to the beach, yet I hate getting sand out of my towel.**

    A simple   C complex

    B compound   D compound-complex

USING VARIED SENTENCE STRUCTURE

To make writing appealing, **use sentences with different structures**. Read the paragraph below.

> I went to my aunt's house this weekend, and I had a good time. My cousins and I played ball, and we also went swimming. We all ate dinner on Sunday, and then my mom came to take me home.

Did you notice that all of the sentences were compound? Did you notice that all of the coordinating conjunctions were *and*? This makes the writing repetitive and a little boring! To add interest to your writing, use different kinds of sentences. Add prepositional phrases and transition words.

PREPOSITIONAL PHRASES

Prepositional phrases add description and interest to a sentence. A prepositional phrase begins with a preposition, like *in, on, with, inside, below,* and so on.

> **Example:** The car <u>with the broken headlight</u> is coming this way.

TRANSITIONAL WORDS

Transitional words are words that link the ideas in two sentences together. Transitions help writing to be smooth. They help readers understand how sentences are related. Transitional words are words like *for example, also, aside from, rather, yet,* and *in other words.*

> **Examples:** Cydney hates going to the doctor, <u>especially</u> when she need to get a shot.
>
> <u>For now</u>, wear the sneakers. <u>Later on</u>, we can buy some dress shoes.

Now, read the same paragraph you saw earlier. This time, it has prepositional phrases and transitional words added.

> I went to my aunt's house in Savannah this weekend. I had a good time with all of my cousins, especially James, who is twelve like me. We played basketball, and we also went swimming in the neighbor's pool. We all ate a delicious picnic dinner outside on Sunday. Finally, my mom came to take me home just as the fireflies were coming out.

What are some of the differences you found? Did you find more details? Were things described more clearly? Can you better see the relationships between the ideas in the paragraph? Did you find a variety in the types of sentences? All of these things can make writing more exciting.

MODIFIERS

Remember to also use **modifiers** in the right way. Modifiers are words and phrases that help describe something in a sentence. They should be close to what they modify.

> **Incorrect:** Tommy unwrapped the presents he got impatiently.

Were the presents given to him impatiently? No, that's how he unwrapped them!

> **Correct:** Tommy impatiently unwrapped the presents he got.

For more practice with modifiers, review chapter 2.

Practice 2:   Using Varied Sentence Structure

Which sentence shows the BEST way to add detail or make the meaning clear?

1

Jennie likes school and gets up early.

A   Jennie likes school in addition to getting up early.

B   Jennie likes school, for example having to get up early.

C   Jennie likes school, aside from having to get up early.

D   Jennie likes school, thus having to get up early.

2

The dog came closer and closer.

A   The dog came closer and closer with the fierce bark.

B   The dog with the fierce bark came closer and closer.

C   The dog within the fierce bark came closer and closer.

D   The fierce bark with the dog came closer and closer.

3

The campsite is the one we are hoping to get.

A   The campsite near the creek is the one we are
hoping to get.

B   The campsite is the one near the creek we are
hoping to get.

C   The campsite is the one we are hoping to get near
the creek.

D   The near the creek campsite is the one we are hoping to get.

4

Put the coat on the chair. I will hang it in the closet.

A   Later on, put the coat on the chair. For now, I will hang it in the closet.

B   Put the coat on the chair. For now later on, I will hang it in the closet.

C   Second, put the coat on the chair. For now, I will hang it in the closet.

D   For now, put the coat on the chair. Later on, I will hang it in the closet.

5

> The wind blew over the umbrella.

A During the night, the wind blew over the umbrella in our yard.

B During the wind in the night the umbrella blew over in our yard.

C The umbrella during the night blew over in the wind.

D In our yard during the night the umbrella was blown.

TYPES OF SENTENCES

There are different kinds of sentences that you can choose from when you write. The four types of sentences are **declarative**, **interrogative**, **imperative**, and **exclamatory**.

Types of Sentences		
Type	**Description**	**Example**
Declarative	states a fact (ends with a period)	Lizards are a type of reptile.
Interrogative	asks a question (ends with a question mark)	Are you going to camp this summer?
Imperative (ends with a period)	gives a command	Stay away from the beehive.
Exclamatory (ends with an exclamation point)	expresses strong feeling	I am so excited that we won the contest!

Use a variety of sentence types to make your writing more interesting.

Practice 3: Types of Sentences

Identify the type of sentence.

1 Jane, would you please pass out the scissors?
   A interrogative   B declarative   C imperative   D exclamatory

2   Why didn't you bring a jacket today?
   A interrogative   B declarative   C imperative   D exclamatory

3   I can't believe your brother locked you out of the bathroom!
   A interrogative   B declarative   C imperative   D exclamatory

4   I am having my birthday party this weekend.
   A interrogative   B declarative   C imperative   D exclamatory

5 **Please put the napkins on the table.**

A   interrogative

B   declarative

C   imperative

D   exclamatory

SENTENCE ERRORS

You have read that there are different types and structures of sentences. Sentences should have variety, but each one needs to be correct.

Here are some common sentence errors.

FRAGMENTS

A **fragment** is part of a sentence. A fragment is missing something that the sentence needs to be complete.

> **Example:** Because the bus had already left.

This is a dependent clause. It cannot stand alone as a sentence. Correct it by adding the missing part. You might write, "Jeremy had to walk to school because the bus had already left."

> **Example:** Plays the drums.

This fragment needs a subject. Correct it by adding the missing part.

You might write, "My cousin plays the drums."

RUN-ONS

A **run-on** has two sentences incorrectly combined into one sentence.

> **Example:** Ariel loves dogs she especially likes golden retrievers.

There are three ways to fix a run-on sentence.

1   Break it into two sentences: Ariel loves dogs. She especially likes golden retrievers.

2   Add a coordinating conjunction and a comma: Ariel loves dogs, but she especially likes golden retrievers.

3   Use a semicolon to separate the two sentences: Ariel loves dogs; she especially likes golden retrievers.

Practice 4:   Sentence Errors

Which sentence is correct?

1 A The light bulb burned out we need a new one.

   B The light bulb burned out; we need a new one.

   C The light bulb burned out and we need a new one.

   D The light bulb burned out, we need a new one.

2 A Blew out the candle.

   B Blew out the candle after the show ended.

   C Juan blew out the candle.

   D Blew out the candle before bed.

3 A If it is not raining.

   B If it is not raining we will.

   C If not raining, we will go.

   D If it is not raining, we'll go to the park after school.

4 A Thanksgiving is always on a Thursday. Easter changes every year.

   B Thanksgiving is always on a Thursday Easter changes every year.

   C Thanksgiving is always on a Thursday; and Easter changes every year.

   D Thanksgiving is always on a Thursday, Easter changes every year.

5 A After they ate dinner.

   B The children helped clear the table after they ate dinner.

   C After they ate dinner and went to bed.

   D After they ate dinner the children.

CHAPTER 5 SUMMARY

Simple, **compound**, **complex**, and **compound-complex** are four **sentence structures**.

Use **prepositional phrases** and **transitional words** to add variety to sentences.

Interrogative, **imperative**, **declarative**, and **exclamatory** are the four types of sentences.

Fragments and **run-ons** are sentence errors and need to be corrected.

CHAPTER 5 REVIEW

A. What structure does each sentence use?

1 **Unless I eat my vegetables, I am not allowed to have dessert.**

    A compound   C compound-complex

    B complex   D simple

2 **A wolf is a carnivore, and a squirrel is an herbivore.**

    A compound   C compound-complex

    B complex   D simple

3 **After falling down the ravine, we waited for help, but no one came for three hours.**

    A compound   C compound-complex

    B complex   D simple

B. Choose the best answer in each set of sentences.

> I did not study for my math test. I got a poor grade.

4 **Which sentence makes the meaning MOST clear?**

    A I did not study for my math test, but I got a poor grade.

    B I did not study for my math test. For instance, I got a poor grade.

    C I did not study for my math test. As a result, I got a poor grade.

    D I did not study for my math test because I got a poor grade.

> The child won the race.

5 **Which sentence shows the BEST way to add detail?**

    A The child in the wheelchair won the race.

    B The child won the race in the wheelchair.

    C In the wheelchair, the child won the race.

    D In the wheelchair, the race was won by the child.

6 **Which sentence is MOST clear?**

   A Ethan is not fond of insects. In particular, he dislikes mosquitoes.

   B Ethan is not fond of insects. He dislikes most mosquitoes.

   C Ethan is not fond of insects; mostly, it's mosquitoes.

   D Ethan is not fond of insects. Mosquitoes are the worst.

C. Identify the type of sentence.

7 **How did the fire start?**

   A interrogative   B declarative   C imperative   D exclamatory

8 **I watched my little brother to help my mom.**

   A interrogative   B declarative   C imperative   D exclamatory

9 **Tie your sneaker during the time out.**

   A interrogative   B declarative   C imperative   D exclamatory

D. Which sentence is correct?

10 A Aside from my sister.

     B Aside from my sister and brother.

     C No one has the password aside from my sister.

     D No one aside from my sister has.

11 A I laced up my skates I fell over immediately.

     B I laced up my skates and I fell over immediately.

     C I laced up my skates but I fell over immediately.

     D I laced up my skates, and I fell over immediately.

12 A Sea Island is their favorite place; they go every summer.

     B Sea Island is their favorite place they go every summer.

     C Sea Island is their favorite place, they go every summer.

     D Sea Island is their favorite place and they go every summer.

Chapter 6
Working with Paragraphs

This chapter covers the following GPS-based CRCT standards:

ELA5C1 The student demonstrates understanding and control of the rules of the English language, realizing that usage involves the appropriate application of conventions and grammar in both written and spoken formats. The student	
b. Expands or reduces sentences (e.g., adding or deleting modifiers, combining or revising sentences).	**c.** Uses and identifies verb phrases and verb tenses.
e. Varies the sentence structure by kind (declarative, interrogative, imperative, and exclamatory sentences and functional fragments), order, and complexity (simple, compound, complex, and compound-complex).	
ELA5W1 The student produces writing that establishes an appropriate organizational structure, sets a context and engages the reader, maintains a coherent focus throughout, and signals a satisfying closure. The student	
a. Selects a focus, an organizational structure, and a point of view based on purpose, genre expectations, audience, length, and format requirements.	**c.** Uses traditional structures for conveying information (e.g., chronological order, cause and effect, similarity and difference, and posing and answering a question).
d. Uses appropriate structures to ensure coherence (e.g., transition elements).	
ELA5W2 The student demonstrates competence in a variety of genres.	
The student produces a <u>narrative</u> that: **a.** Creates an organizing structure.	The student produces <u>informational</u> writing (e.g., report, procedures, correspondence) that: **b.** Develops a controlling idea that conveys a perspective on a subject.
c. Creates an organizing structure appropriate to a specific purpose, audience, and context.	The student produces a <u>persuasive</u> essay that: **d.** Creates an organizing structure appropriate to a specific purpose, audience, and context.
ELA5W4 The student consistently uses a writing process to develop, revise, and evaluate writing. The student	
b. Revises manuscripts to improve the meaning and focus of writing by adding, deleting, consolidating, clarifying, and rearranging words and sentences.	

REVISING PARAGRAPHS

In chapter 5, you read about sentences. Now, let's look at combining sentences into paragraphs. A **paragraph** is a group of sentences that focuses on a topic. Each paragraph has one main idea. Think about how to put together sentences so that your ideas are clear and interesting.

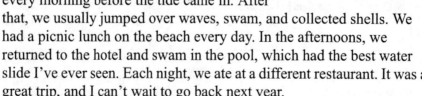

COMBINING SENTENCES

Some paragraphs are clearer and more interesting than others. Read the paragraph below.

> My mom, dad, grandpa, and sister all went to the beach for a week this summer. We all had a good time. We built sand castles. We jumped over waves. We swam in the ocean. We collected shells. We built a sand castle every morning. We swam in the hotel pool. The pool had a water slide. We had a picnic lunch on the beach every day. We ate in a restaurant every night. It was a great trip. We were there for a week. Everyone had a good time.

Notice how the paragraph contains many short sentences. The sentences are all similar in structure; most start with "we." A few ideas, like building the sand castle and the fact that the trip was for a week are repeated.

In chapter 5, you read about using a sentence variety. This means using different sentence types and structures. When you revise a paragraph, look at the sentences. Are they all the same? Do any repeat ideas? Can you change some to make them more interesting? To improve the paragraph you just read, the writer revised it to **combine sentences** and **take out repeated ideas**.

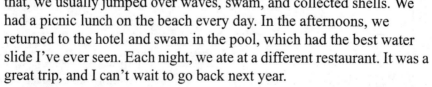

> My mom, dad, grandpa, and sister all went to the beach for a week this summer. Everyone had such a good time! We built a sand castle every morning before the tide came in. After that, we usually jumped over waves, swam, and collected shells. We had a picnic lunch on the beach every day. In the afternoons, we returned to the hotel and swam in the pool, which had the best water slide I've ever seen. Each night, we ate at a different restaurant. It was a great trip, and I can't wait to go back next year.

Notice the revisions to this paragraph. Some sentences have been combined to add interest and variety. Some sentences have been reworded. There are now transition words and different types of sentences. Ideas are no longer repeated.

As you combine sentences, be sure to use correct **punctuation** and **mechanics**. Review chapters 3 and 5 for more about how to do that.

CONSISTENT VERB TENSE

You read in chapter 2 that it is important to **keep verb tense consistent** in a sentence. It is also important to keep verb tense consistent in a paragraph. Doing so helps your ideas to be clear to your reader.

Read the following paragraph. It is the same paragraph from page 70. What do you notice about the verbs?

> My mom, dad, grandpa, and sister all went to the beach for a week this summer. Everyone has such a good time! We are building a sand castle every morning before the tide came in. After that, we usually jumped over waves, were swimming, and collect shells. We had a picnic lunch on the beach every day. In the afternoons, we return to the hotel and swim in the pool, which had the best water slide I've ever seen. Each night, we eat at a different restaurant. It was a great trip, and I can't wait to go back next year.

You may notice that the verbs in this sentence jump around. Some are in the past tense, and some are in the present tense. When writing a paragraph, it is important to keep verb tense consistent. Choose a tense and stick with it.

POINT OF VIEW

All writing has a **point of view**. This shows who is telling what happened. Here are the types of point of view.

Two Types of Point of View		
Point of View	**First Person**	**Third Person**
Narrator	character, whether named or unnamed	unknown identity
Pronoun signals	*I, my, mine, we, our, ours*	*he, she, they, them, their, theirs,* or no pronouns
Example	I turned on the lights. That's when everyone yelled "Surprise!" All my friends were there, and we had so much fun.	The mountain range stretches for many miles. In the pioneer days, travelers had a hard time crossing it.

When you write, you have to decide how to talk to your audience. Should a character tell what happened? This is usually the case when you write a story. Other times, you may write factual information that doesn't really have a person telling it. This can be the case in reports or articles. No matter what you decide, be consistent with your point of view.

CLARITY

Clarity refers how well a reader can tell what you are saying. It is important to make your ideas clear to your audience. We all want to be understood. Putting sentences together in a way that makes sense helps to make your meaning clear.

Read the paragraph on page 71 again. What do you notice about the clarity?

The ideas about what the family did are all there, but the order of the sentences doesn't make much sense. For example, the writer talks about dinner, then jumps back to afternoons. The day seems all jumbled up. A clearer way to write this would be to use the order in which events happened. When deciding on which sentence to put where, think about what makes the most sense.

Practice 1: Revising Paragraphs

Answer the questions about revising paragraphs.

> [1]Goldfish are good pets. [2]Goldfish do not greet you at the door. [3]They do not hop onto your lap. [4]They are not cuddly. [5]Goldfish are not as much work as dogs and cats. [6]They don't eat much, and they did not need walks. [7]They are easy to clean up after. [8]They don't make any noise. [9]They eat very little. [10]They are fun to watch and good company when you are reading a book. [11]Some people say that goldfish do not make good pets.

1 **Which sentence in the paragraph below repeats an idea?**

   A sentence 2

   B sentence 8

   C sentence 9

   D sentence 11

2 **What would be the BEST way to combine sentences 3 and 4?**

   A They do not hop onto your lap, they are not cuddly.

   B They are not cuddly and do not hop onto your lap.

   C They do not hop onto your lap, aren't cuddly either.

   D They are not cuddly or hop onto your lap.

3 **What is the BEST way to make the verb tense in sentence 6 consistent?**

A They don't eat much, and they don't need walks.

B They did not eat much, and they did not need walks.

C They don't eat much, and they are not needing walks.

D They are not eating much or needing walks.

4 **Which two sentences should change places for clarity?**

A sentence 1 and sentence 2

B sentence 2 and sentence 10

C sentence 1 and sentence 11

D sentence 9 and sentence 11

5 **What point of view does this paragraph use?**

A first person

B third person

6 **What would be the BEST transition word to start sentence 5?**

A Meanwhile,

B For example,

C Afterward,

D However,

ORGANIZING PARAGRAPHS

When writing a paragraph, you need to organize your ideas. **Organizing a paragraph** makes it more effective. It also helps readers to understand what is going on. In this section, you will read about four ways to organize. Each one is used for a different purpose. You need to think about your **focus** and your **audience** to choose the right one.

CHRONOLOGICAL ORDER

Chronological order is the order in which things happen. A paragraph that follows chronological order talks about events in the order that they occurred.

The paragraph below is organized in chronological order.

> Every Saturday morning, my family has the same routine. My brother and I get up first. We watch cartoons or read until 8:30 a.m. Then, we start making a big, deluxe breakfast. We make food like scrambled eggs, grits, cinnamon toast, and waffles. When it is ready, we wake my dad up. We eat as much as we want, and then Dad cleans up the kitchen.

A **narrative** (story) also usually uses chronological order. In a narrative, you don't have to tell the events in the order they happened. You can skip around and use flashbacks and other time devices.

TRANSITIONS IN CHRONOLOGICAL ORDER PARAGRAPHS

You read about **transitional words and phrases** in chapter 5. You can use transitions in paragraphs to show how ideas relate to one another. Some transitions that are often used in chronological paragraphs are *soon*, *meanwhile*, *later*, *today*, *then*, and *next*.

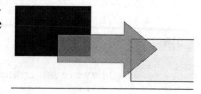

CAUSE AND EFFECT

Cause and effect paragraphs look at the relationships between ideas. Sometimes they focus more on what made an event happen (the cause). Sometimes they focus more on the result of the event (the effect).

The paragraph below is organized to show cause and effect.

> Dentists always say, "Brush your teeth!" Brushing your teeth often and correctly helps to keep your teeth and gums healthy. Brushing removes plaque, so it helps prevent cavities. Brushing also helps to remove odors from our breath, especially after eating. Now doctors are saying that brushing even protects against infections and heart problems.

This paragraph focuses on the effects of brushing your teeth.

TRANSITIONS IN CAUSE AND EFFECT PARAGRAPHS

Some transitions that are often used in cause and effect paragraphs are *due to*, *because of*, *consequently*, and *so*.

COMPARE AND CONTRAST

A **compare and contrast** paragraph looks at how things are alike and different. If you focus on how they are alike (similarities), you are comparing. If you focus on how they are different, you are contrasting. Some paragraphs look at both how things are alike and different.

The paragraph below is organized to compare and contrast.

Apples and bananas are both healthy fruits. However, they have several differences. First, an apple must be washed. Then, you can eat its skin. A banana does not have to be washed, but it must be peeled. The peel is not edible. Apples come in many shapes, colors, and even flavors. The bananas we see at the market are mostly one kind—yellow! Finally, an apple is messier to eat than a banana, since apples are juicy. A banana is not really messy to eat, but you do need to find a place to throw away the peel.

This paragraph focuses on contrasting apples to bananas.

TRANSITIONS IN COMPARE AND CONTRAST PARAGRAPHS

Some transitions that are often used to compare are *like*, *just as*, and *also*. Some transitions that are often used to contrast include *however*, *but*, and *even though*.

QUESTION AND ANSWER

A **question and answer** paragraph poses a question then answers that question.

The paragraph below is organized using question and answer.

> Everyone seems to be talking about going green. I wondered what I, an eleven-year-old kid, could do to go green and help the earth. I thought of two things I can do. First, I can recycle. I have many school projects, and things like cereal boxes that we normally throw out would be good for those projects. I can also use my allowance to buy my mom one of those reusable grocery bags. They are not expensive, and they will help us not use so many plastic bags. In fact, these are two easy things that will help me go green.

In this paragraph, the writer poses a question then provides answers (or solutions).

TRANSITIONS IN QUESTION AND ANSWER PARAGRAPHS

Some transitions that are often used in question and answer paragraphs are *for this reason*, *in fact*, and *with this in mind*.

Practice 2: Organization

Read the paragraphs, and answer the questions that follow.

^{1}My cousin's family is deciding where to go on vacation. ^{2}My cousin Joe wants to go to the mountains. ^{3}He says that in the mountains there will be plenty of nature and privacy. ^{4}Joe's stepmother wants to go to New York City. ^{5}Joe says that New York will be hot, noisy, and crowded. ^{6}The two places they are talking about are very different. ^{7}I think they will have a hard time deciding between the two.

1 **The previous paragraph is an example of what organizational structure?**

A chronological order

B cause and effect

C compare and contrast

D question and answer

2 **Which transition would BEST connect sentences 3 and 4?**

A On the other hand,

B At the same time,

C Next,

D Later,

[1]When cooking pasta, it is important to follow the steps in just the right order. [2]Bring a pot of salted water to a boil. [3]Next, add the pasta. [4]Set the timer. [5]Stir the pasta occasionally. [6]While the pasta cooks, heat the sauce. [7]When the pasta is done, drain the water, put on the sauce, and top it with cheese. [8]Then, enjoy it!

3 **This paragraph is an example of what organizational structure?**

A chronological order

B cause and effect

C compare and contrast

D question and answer

4 **Which transition would BEST connect sentences 1 and 2?**

A Instead,

B First,

C Then,

D In fact,

[1]On Tuesday, I was late to school, even though I got up on time. [2]While I was getting dressed, I realized I did not have any clean socks, so I had to borrow some from my brother. [3]Because I took so long getting dressed, Mom said I did not have time for breakfast, so I had to take a piece of toast to eat on the way to school. [4]Then, while I was walking to school, a dog smelled my toast and chased me, so I had to run three blocks out of my way. [5]I was late, even though I woke up when I was supposed to.

5 **This paragraph is an example of what organizational structure?**

A chronological order

C compare and contrast

B cause and effect

D question and answer

6 **Which transition would BEST connect sentences 4 and 5?**

A With this in mind,

C Consequently,

B Also,

D But,

MAIN IDEA

A good paragraph focuses on making a point. The **main idea** of a paragraph is what the paragraph is about. All of the sentences in a paragraph support the main idea or main point.

Read the paragraph below.

Aaron loves to ride his bike. As soon as he gets home from school, he grabs his bike and rides up and down the street a few times. When he finishes his homework, he rides to his friend Sam's house, and then the two of them are gone until dinner. On weekends, Aaron is gone almost all day, exploring all streets near his house. He likes how quiet bike riding is and how much he can see by riding slowly.

The main idea of the paragraph is that Aaron loves to ride his bike. All of the details in the paragraph prove that this is true.

When determining the main idea of a paragraph, ask yourself, "What is the point of this paragraph?" The answer is usually the main idea. When you write, be sure each paragraph has one main idea.

Practice 3: Main Idea

Read each paragraph.

Julio needs to get more exercise. In his free time, he likes to watch TV, play video games, and talk with his friends. For most of these activities, Julio does not need to move. He is starting to gain weight. He also has little energy. Finding more active ways to spend his time will help Julio get the exercise he need.

1 **Which sentence BEST states the main idea of the paragraph?**

A Julio gets too much exercise.

B Julio watches too much TV.

C Julio needs to get more exercise.

D Julio should never play video games.

Can you imagine being able to travel in time? Time travel would be an adventure. It would be a way to see the past and the future. It might be dangerous, but it would definitely be interesting. I can't wait until someone invents a way to travel through time.

2 Which sentence BEST states the main idea of the paragraph?

A   Time travel is an old idea.

B   It is a good thing there is no time travel.

C   No one has invented time travel yet.

D   It would be exciting to be able to travel in time.

Roderick has beautiful table manners. He always keeps his napkin in his lap, chews with his mouth closed, and waits until he has swallowed to speak. His parents appreciate his good manners. They can't wait until Roderick's baby sister can do the same.

3 Which sentence BEST states the main idea of the paragraph?

A   Roderick has good table manners.

B   Roderick chews with his mouth closed.

C   Roderick's sister has bad manners.

D   Roderick's parents are proud of him.

Basketball requires many different skills. Players need to be able to think quickly, plan ahead, and move fast. Good players control the ball and their movements. They look for ways to support their teammates and score points. It takes many different skills to be a good basketball player.

4 Which sentence BEST states the main idea of the paragraph?

A   Slow people should not try to play basketball.

B   A good basketball player uses many skills.

C   Boys are better at basketball than girls.

D   Basketball is all about scoring points.

> ### CHAPTER 6 SUMMARY
>
> Revise paragraphs to make them more effective. You can do this by **combining sentences, keeping verbs consistent,** and **putting sentences in a logical order.**
>
> **Organize paragraphs** so they are clear. Use **chronological order, cause and effect, compare and contrast,** and **question and answer.**
>
> Use **transitions** in paragraphs to show how ideas are related.
>
> The **main idea** of a paragraph is what a paragraph is about.

CHAPTER 6 REVIEW

Answer the questions about revising paragraphs.

¹I have some friends whose parents don't let them watch TV. ²The parents say that TV is a waste of time. ³They think their kids should be doing something productive instead. ⁴I agree that some TV programs are a waste of time. ⁵I thought that TV can sometimes be a good thing. ⁶Now I make dinner once a week for my whole family. ⁷For example, I have learned how to cook by watching cooking shows. ⁸TV doesn't have to be bad. ⁹It can actually teach you new things. ¹⁰Some TV programs are a waste of time.

1   Which two sentences should change places for clarity?

A   sentences 1 and 6

B   sentences 2 and 8

C   sentences 7 and 1

D   sentences 6 and 7

2   What would be the BEST transition word to start sentence 5?

A   For example,

B   However,

C   Then,

D   Consequently,

3   **What point of view does this paragraph use?**

A   first person

B   third person

4   **Which sentence in the paragraph below repeats an idea?**

A   sentence 2

B   sentence 5

C   sentence 7

D   sentence 10

5   **What would be the BEST way to combine sentences 8 and 9?**

A   TV doesn't have to be bad, it can actually teach you new things.

B   TV doesn't have to be bad; it can actually teach you new things.

C   TV doesn't have to be bad, but it can actually teach you new things.

D   TV doesn't have to be bad and it can actually teach you new things.

6   **What is the BEST way to make the verb tense in sentence 5 consistent?**

A   I will be thinking that TV can sometimes be a good thing.

B   I am thinking that TV can sometimes be a good thing.

C   I had thought that TV can sometimes be a good thing.

D   I think that TV can sometimes be a good thing.

[1]My brother has sucked his thumb since he was a baby. [2]My mom says it has caused problems with his mouth. [3]His teeth don't come together as they should. [4]He has a hard time saying *s* words. [5]He will probably need braces when he is older due to his thumb-sucking.

7   **This paragraph is an example of what organizational structure?**

A   chronological order

B   cause and effect

C   compare and contrast

D   question and answer

8 **Which transition would BEST begin sentence 4?**

A Then,

B Later,

C Instead,

D As a result,

[1]When you make a bed, it is important to follow all of the steps. [2]You need to put the fitted sheet on first. [3]Then, you top it with the flat sheet. [4]Blankets and quilts go on top of that. [5]Add the pillows. Finally, your bed is made!

9 **This paragraph is an example of what organizational structure?**

A cause and effect

B chronological order

C question and answer

D compare and contrast

10 **Which transition would BEST begin sentence 5?**

A First,

B Last,

C Especially,

D Meanwhile,

[1]Being a gymnast is hard work. [2]If I want to be good, I need to practice often. [3]I practice four days each week, and in the summer I practice five days each week. [4]I run to build up my strength. [5]I take ballet to build my coordination. [6]Gymnastics is tiring and does not leave much time for other things.

11 **Which sentence BEST states the main idea of this paragraph?**

A   Being a gymnast is easy.

B   Ballet is more important than gymnastics.

C   Runners make good gymnasts.

D   It is hard work to be a gymnast.

[1]My cat, Simon, is a troublemaker. [2]He hops on the counter and eats out of my cereal bowl. [3]He drinks out of the toilet. [4]He even scratches holes in our screen door. [5]It's a good thing we all love him!

12 **Which sentence BEST states the main idea of the paragraph?**

A   Simon gets sick from eating people food.

B   Simon is a troublemaker.

C   Simon is a good cat.

D   Simon helps me eat my breakfast.

Chapter 7
Writing Essays

This chapter covers the following GPS-based CRCT standards:

ELA5W1 The student produces writing that establishes an appropriate organizational structure, sets a context and engages the reader, maintains a coherent focus throughout, and signals a satisfying closure. The student	
b. Writes texts of a length appropriate to address the topic or tell the story.	
ELA5W2 The student demonstrates competence in a variety of genres.	
The student produces a <u>narrative</u> that: **d.** Includes sensory details and concrete language to develop plot and character.	**e.** Excludes extraneous details and inconsistencies.
The student produces <u>informational</u> writing (e.g., report, procedures, correspondence) that: **d.** Includes appropriate facts and details.	**e.** Excludes extraneous details and inappropriate information.
The student produces a <u>response</u> to <u>literature</u> that: **a.** Engages the reader by establishing a context, creating a speaker's voice, and otherwise developing reader interest.	**c.** Supports judgments through references to the text, other works, authors, or non-print media, or references to personal knowledge.
e. Excludes extraneous details and inappropriate information.	The student produces a <u>persuasive essay</u> that: **a.** Engages the reader by establishing a context, creating a speaker's voice, and otherwise developing reader interest.
b. States a clear position in support of a proposal.	**c.** Supports a position with relevant evidence.
e. Addresses reader concerns.	**f.** Excludes extraneous details and inappropriate information.
ELA5W4 The student consistently uses a writing process to develop, revise, and evaluate writing. The student	
a. Plans and drafts independently and resourcefully.	**b.** Revises manuscripts to improve the meaning and focus of writing by adding, deleting, consolidating, clarifying, and rearranging words and sentences.
c. Edits to correct errors in spelling, punctuation, etc.	

An **essay** is a short piece of writing about one topic. In an essay, a writer might do one of the following:

- Describe how to do something.
- Give information.
- Tell about a personal experience.
- Argue for or against something.

The CRCT does not require you to write an essay. (You will write an essay in a separate test, the Georgia grade 5 Writing Assessment.) But, you will need to know about different kinds of essays, what to put in an essay, and how to organize it. The best way to recognize what makes a good essay is to know how to write one yourself. Let's begin by looking at different kinds of essays.

ESSAY GENRES

There are a few different kinds of essays you might write in school and see on the CRCT.

NARRATIVE

A **narrative essay** tells a story. For example, if your language arts teacher asked you to write an essay about your last family vacation, that would be a narrative essay.

INFORMATIONAL

The purpose of an **informational essay** is to teach. For example, you might write an informational essay in a science class that describes the life cycle of a frog.

Frog Life Cycle

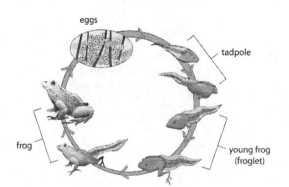

RESPONSE TO LITERATURE

This type of essay is written after reading literature. For example, your teacher may ask you to compare two poems. Your **response to literature** essay might talk about what is the same in the two poems.

PERSUASIVE

A **persuasive essay** states an opinion on an issue. The writer uses facts and other proof to persuade the reader to see the issue as the writer does. For example, you might write a persuasive essay in social studies class about why you think people should vote for a certain politician.

POINT OF VIEW

In persuasive writing, you are telling your **point of view**. As you know, the term *point of view* can mean "an opinion." It can also mean who is telling the information (the narrator). When writing a persuasive essay, you need to think about both!

Maybe you want to e-mail your mom asking for permission to buy a new video game. In this case, you would use the **first-person point of view**. This means you might say, "*I* think *I* should be able to buy this new game. Here is why."

Sometimes, it is better not to write in first person. Many persuasive essays use the **third-person point of view** to focus on facts, not who is telling them. Instead of "*I* think speeding is dangerous," you would write "Speeding is dangerous." Taking *I* out of the essay can make it more persuasive. It is easier to convince a reader with proof (like facts about speeding) than with your own personal opinion.

Practice 1: Essay Genres

1 Which type of essay would be BEST for writing about the solar system?

 A narrative   C response to literature

 B informational   D persuasive

2 Which type of essay would be BEST for writing about your opinion of school uniforms?

 A narrative   C response to literature

 B informational   D persuasive

3 Which type of essay would be BEST for writing about your first day of school?

 A narrative   C response to literature

 B informational   D persuasive

4 Which of the following is an example of persuasive writing in the third-person point of view?

 A I think we need healthier school lunches at Brighton Elementary.

 B Better meals will give me more energy so I can study hard.

 C Schools can help children learn healthy eating habits by offering healthy foods.

 D I like hamburgers, and the school should serve them more often.

5   Which of these sentences gives the BEST proof to a reader?

A   I like to blend in with everyone else.

B   I think school uniforms are a good idea.

C   I don't like to waste time choosing my clothes each morning.

D   Studies show that students who wear uniforms earn higher grades.

WRITING AN ESSAY

THE WRITING PROCESS

When you write an essay, you follow certain steps. This is called the **writing process**. Its steps help you to create an effective essay.

Step 1: Plan
The first step when starting an essay is to **plan**. Choosing a topic, brainstorming, and outlining are all part of the planning step.
Step 2: Draft
The second step is to **draft**. In this step, the writer creates a rough version of the essay. The key is to fill in all the details needed to explain the topic.
Step 3: Revise
The third step is to **revise**. In this step, the writer looks for ways to make meaning clearer. This could include adding details, moving around parts of the essay, deleting sentences, and rearranging words.
Step 4: Proofread
The fourth step is to **proofread**. In this step, the writer corrects errors in spelling, punctuation, and word usage.

ORGANIZING

An essay needs to have **logical organization** to be clear. Each paragraph of the essay should be structured in a way that helps a reader understand the writer's ideas. Each part of a paragraph works with the other parts to make the writer's meaning clear.

A **topic sentence** tells what the paragraph will be about. It is often the first sentence in the paragraph. This sentence gives the reader a preview of what a paragraph will talk about.

Example: E-mail is a better way to communicate than regular mail.

After reading this topic sentence, **supporting sentences** need to provide details. The reader would expect to be told how e-mail is better than regular mail. The sentences that follow would give reasons, facts, details, and examples to support the topic sentence and show that it is true.

> **Example:** E-mail is free, but stamps for regular mail are getting more and more expensive. E-mail is quicker. An e-mail takes minutes to arrive, but regular mail takes days to arrive.

Notice how each supporting sentence sticks to the topic. Every detail and example points back to the topic sentence.

The final sentence of the paragraph is the **closing sentence**. A closing sentence sums up the paragraph.

> **Example:** In all, e-mail is the quicker, cheaper way to write to people.

Notice how the closing sentence restates the main idea of the sentence. It should not use the exact words, though. It should also not introduce any new ideas.

Here is how the complete paragraph would look.

E-mail is a better way to communicate than regular mail. E-mail is free, but stamps for regular mail are getting more and more expensive. E-mail is also quicker. An e-mail takes minutes to arrive, but regular mail takes days to arrive. In all, e-mail is the quicker, cheaper way to write to people.

WHAT TO INCLUDE

What kind of information you include in an essay depends upon what kind of essay you are writing. You need to **include details and arguments** that help make your point.

A **narrative essay** should include many details. You will want to use language that is specific and descriptive. The details in a narrative should help a reader see, hear, smell, taste, and feel what is going on. They should also make the plot easy to follow. Finally, they should help us to see and know the characters.

> **Example:** The boy looked very unusual. On his head, he wore a knitted cap with a jingling bell attached to the top. His shirt had spangles in the shape of a star. His pants were red denim. But the strangest thing was the sneer on his face, which didn't match the childish style of his clothing.

Notice the use of adjectives and other descriptive language in this narrative passage. Giving details is important in narrative writing.

An **informative essay** should include many facts and examples.

> **Example:** When honey bees are alarmed, they sting. The bees die when they sting. Worker bees have a stinger and a venom sac. When the bee stings, the stinger and sac pull free from the bee. This kills the bee.

Notice the use of facts to give information about the topic.

A **response to literature** should include things that will keep a reader's interest. There should be reference to the literature. The writer might discuss other works or relate these ideas to what he already knows.

> **Example:** *Little House on the Prairie* gives the reader an idea of how pioneers actually lived. It tells about the kinds of houses they lived in, what they ate, how they cooked, and what they did for fun. Today, children do some of the same activities that Laura and Mary did. However, most children today are not responsible for as many chores as these girls were.

Notice how the response to literature passage talks about the book the writer is responding to. This passage shows the writer relating ideas from the book to the world she knows.

A **persuasive essay** should include support for the writer's position. The writer would use proof that supports his point. However, he should also acknowledge his readers' concerns.

> **Example:** Schools should be allowed to sell candy. Candy sales are important fundraising activities for schools. I know some parents might not like this, but kids can get candy anywhere. Why not support the school with that money?

Notice how the writer supports his belief with reasons in this persuasive passage. He also addresses a possible objection from people who do not share his point of view.

WHAT NOT TO INCLUDE

When you include the right kinds of information in an essay, you build a strong essay. In the same way, you will want to **remove information that doesn't help** build a strong essay. When revising your writing, look closely at your words and ideas. You will want to remove the following:

- details that don't matter
- facts that don't support your point
- information that is distracting to the reader
- information that disproves your point

> **Example:** Schools should be allowed to sell candy. Candy causes cavities. Candy sales are important fundraising activities for schools. I know some parents might not like this, but kids can get candy anywhere. Why not support the school with that money?

Do you see a new sentence that does not help the writer's point? "Candy causes cavities" may be true, but it actually hurts the writer's point. This sentence should be removed to create stronger writing.

Practice 2: Writing an Essay

Read the paragraphs below. Then answer the questions.

1 **Which of the following is the BEST topic sentence for this paragraph?**

> My aunt learned how to paint her house after she watched a home show. My mom used recipes from a cooking show to make Thanksgiving dinner. My little brother even learned his letters by watching *Sesame Street*. I think that if you watch the right kind of shows, TV can be useful.

A All television shows are bad.

B Television has a bad reputation but can actually be quite educational.

C I love to watch TV, and I have four favorite shows I watch all the time.

D Doctors say TV is bad for young kids.

2 **Which supporting detail is MOST important to add to the paragraph below?**

> Paris is a city everyone should visit. There are old, historic buildings to explore. Some of the best art museums in the world are in Paris. The food is delicious as well. Paris is famous for its fresh bread and delicious desserts. It is definitely a place to see at least once in your life!

A Plane tickets to Paris are expensive, but the trip will be worth it.

B In Paris, people speak French.

C It is easy to get lost.

D You can take a picnic lunch to one of the many public gardens.

3 **Which is the BEST closing sentence for the paragraph below?**

> It is easier than people think to grow vegetables. You can start with either seeds or small plants. You will plant these in rich, loose soil. Add sunlight and the right amount of water, and soon your plants will be growing. After a few weeks or so, your crop will be ready.

A With just a little work, you can grow your own food.

B Sometimes the plants don't grow.

C Peas are my favorite vegetable.

D I have never tried to grow fruit, but I want to.

4 **Which sentence should be removed from the paragraph below?**

> There are many ways to make a sandwich more interesting. Instead of the same old turkey or ham, why not use leftover chicken? You can use a tortilla instead of bread or even serve the sandwich in bites on crackers. Desserts can be a healthy way to end your meal. Some people like grilled vegetable sandwiches. By thinking about what you like and how you could make it into a sandwich, you can create all kinds of original lunches!

A Instead of the same old turkey or ham, why not use leftover chicken?

B Some people like grilled vegetable sandwiches.

C Desserts can be a healthy way to end your meal.

D You can use a tortilla instead of bread or even serve the sandwich in bites on crackers.

5 **In which step of the essay would a writer delete sentences and move paragraphs around?**

A Step 1: Plan

B Step 2: Draft

C Step 3: Revise

D Step 4: Proofread

CHAPTER 7 SUMMARY

Narrative essays tell a story. **Informational essays** teach. **Response to literature essays** discuss literature. **Persuasive essays** argue a point.

The **steps of the writing process** are plan, draft, revise, and proofread.

A well-organized paragraph has a **topic sentence, supporting sentences**, and a **concluding sentence**.

Essays should include information that **supports** the writer's ideas and points. Writers should **remove** information that does not do this.

CHAPTER 7 REVIEW

1 **Which type of essay would be BEST for writing about how to set up a computer?**

  A narrative

  B informational

  C response to literature

  D persuasive

2 **In which step of the essay would a writer decide on the topic for an essay?**

  A Step 1: Plan

  B Step 2: Draft

  C Step 3: Revise

  D Step 4: Proofread

3 **Which type of essay would be BEST for writing about your family's holiday traditions?**

  A narrative

  B informational

  C response to literature

  D persuasive

4   **Which of the following is an example of persuasive writing in third-person point of view?**

A   I think that bike helmets are a smart idea.

B   I have seen bike helmets that are stylish.

C   Studies have shown that bike helmets save lives.

D   I like my bike helmet which has red stars on it.

After reading the paragraph below, answer questions 5 and 6.

> Making a bookmark is a fun and easy project. Bookmarks are a thoughtful, homemade gift that nearly everyone can use. You can start with any type and color of paper, though stiff paper will work best. Decorate the bookmark with markers, stickers, pictures cut from magazines, or even photographs. Bookmarks are inexpensive to buy at the store. To make the bookmark last longer, cover it in clear contact paper.

5   **Which supporting detail is MOST important to add to the paragraph?**

A   You can write a message on a bookmark and even add glitter.

B   Bookmarks take a long time to make.

C   Some people don't like paper projects since it takes a lot of work.

D   Bookmarks might hurt people's feelings.

6   **Which sentence should be removed from the paragraph?**

A   Making a bookmark is a fun and easy project.

B   Bookmarks are inexpensive to buy at the store.

C   To make the bookmark last longer, cover it in clear contact paper.

D   You can start with any type and color of paper, though stiff paper will work best.

After reading the paragraph below, answer questions 7 and 8.

> If you are ever lost in the woods, knowing how to make a shelter, find water, build a fire, and get food can save your life. It is important to walk into the woods prepared for the unexpected. This includes having the right tools and skills to take care of yourself. Organizations like the Boy Scouts and the Girl Scouts teach songs and crafts. Being prepared helps you to stay safe.

7 **Which of the following is the BEST topic sentence for this paragraph?**

A   The forest can be confusing because trees can look the same.

B   Hiking is a relaxing hobby.

C   Wilderness survival skills can save your life.

D   Forest fires are dangerous.

8 **Which sentence should be removed from the paragraph?**

A   It is important to walk into the woods prepared for the unexpected.

B   Being prepared helps you to stay safe.

C   This includes having the right tools and skills to take care of yourself.

D   Organizations like the Boy Scouts and the Girl Scouts teach songs and crafts.

After reading the paragraph below, answer questions 9 and 10.

> Tide pools contain many kinds of animals. Snails, sea anemones, and fish are some of the living creatures you can find in a tide pool. Waves crashing on the rocks at the seashore leave water behind. This water makes a home for all kinds of interesting wildlife. Last summer, I found a starfish in a tide pool. My brother made the mistake of trying to catch a crab.

9 **Which is the BEST closing sentence for the paragraph?**

A   He learned the hard way not to touch some creatures that live in tide pools.

B   Starfish have five arms and can even regrow an arm.

C   A trip to the beach can be educational.

D   More people should try to catch sea creatures.

10 **Which supporting detail is MOST important to add to the paragraph?**

A   I love going to the beach to hunt for shells.

B   Everyone should wear sunblock near the ocean.

C   Tide pools are found in the rocky areas next to the ocean's edge.

D   Watch out for rip tides when swimming in the ocean.

Chapter 8
Research

This chapter covers the following GPS-based CRCT standards:

ELA5W2 The student demonstrates competence in a variety of genres.	
The student produces a <u>narrative</u> that: **i.** Lifts the level of language using appropriate strategies including word choice. The student produces <u>informational</u> writing (e.g., report, procedures, correspondence) that: **i.** Lifts the level of language using appropriate strategies including word choice.	The student produces a <u>response to literature</u> that: **g.** Lifts the level of language using appropriate strategies including word choice.
The student produces a <u>persuasive essay</u> that: **h.** Raises the level of language using appropriate strategies (word choice).	
ELA5W3 The student uses research and technology to support writing. The student	
a. Acknowledges information from sources.	**b.** Uses organizational features of printed text (i.e., citations, end notes, bibliographic references, appendices) to locate relevant information.
c. Uses various reference materials (i.e., dictionary, thesaurus, encyclopedia, electronic information, almanac, atlas, magazines, newspapers) as aids to writing.	**d.** Uses the features of texts (e.g., index, table of contents, guide words, alphabetical/numerical order) to obtain and organize information and thoughts.
e. Demonstrates basic keyboarding skills and familiarity with computer terminology (e.g., software, memory, disk drive, hard drive).	**g.** Uses a thesaurus to identify alternative word choices and meanings.
ELA5W4 The student consistently uses a writing process to develop, revise, and evaluate writing. The student	
b. Revises manuscripts to improve the meaning and focus of writing by adding, deleting, consolidating, clarifying, and rearranging words and sentences.	

DOING RESEARCH

What do you do when you want to learn about something? You might ask a teacher. You might read a book. You might use a computer. When you do these things, you are researching. When you do **research**, you find out about a topic. For example, if you wanted to find out more than you already know about horses, you could research them.

TYPES OF RESEARCH SOURCES

There are many different tools you can use to do research. You might look for more information using an encyclopedia, a computer, or a book about horses. The **types of research sources** you use depend on what you want to know. If you wanted to learn the name of a mountain range in South America, you would use one type of source. If you wanted to learn about the war in Iraq, you would use a different type of source.

The table below shows different kinds of sources.

Research Sources		
Source	**Description**	**Examples**
Internet	a collection of resources accessed with a computer	www.nasa.gov, www.wikipedia.org
magazine	a publication that is published on a regular schedule that contains pictures and articles	*National Geographic Kids*, *TIME*
encyclopedia	a book or series of books with articles on many different topics	*DK Children's Illustrated Encyclopedia*
newspaper	a daily or weekly publication that is a source of current news	*The Atlanta Journal-Constitution, USA Today*
almanac	a once-a-year publication that tells about weather and events on a calendar	*Old Farmer's Almanac, CIA World Factbook*
keywords	words used in a search for information in libraries or online; keywords	horses, wild horses, ponies
atlas	book containing maps and other geographic information	world atlas, historical atlas

PARTS OF BOOKS

Knowing about the **parts of books** also can help you find information. Most reference books have certain sections. They can help you find what you are looking for in the book or to learn more about certain words in the book.

Parts of a Reference Book		
Part	**Description**	**Example**
table of contents	a list at the start of a book showing what is in it, including chapters and page numbers	Chapter 3: How Horses Came to America.........page 26
index	a list in the back of a book with topics found in the book and what page they are on	palomino horses......page 73
glossary	a list of words used in the book and their definitions	mane: the long hair that grows on the head and neck of a horse

Practice 1: Doing Research

Use the chart titled Research Sources to answer questions 1 through 4.

1   Which source would be BEST for finding out which countries border Italy?

   A   an almanac

   B   a world atlas

   C   a magazine about Italian cooking

   D   the keyword Italy typed into a search engine

2   Which source would be BEST for finding many articles about your favorite band?

   A   a historical atlas

   B   a daily newspaper

   C   the Internet

   D   an encyclopedia

3   Which source would be BEST to find out who won the World Series of baseball in a certain year?

   A   an encyclopedia

   B   an atlas of the United States

   C   an entertainment magazine

   D   a sports almanac

4   Which source would be BEST for reading about how your local football team did yesterday?

   A   a newspaper

   B   a magazine

   C   an almanac

   D   an encyclopedia

Look at these sections from a book. Then, answer the questions that follow.

Table of Contents

Glossary

wean – to get a child or young animal to begin eating other food in place of its mother's milk

weasel – a mammal with brown fur and a long, slender body

wetlands – land where water covers the soil; it is home to many types of animals

wing – a limb on a bird, covered with feathers, that a bird uses to fly

5   On which page would you find information about flamingoes?

A   143

B   152

C   31

D   19

6 In which chapter would you find information about fish?

A Chapter 2

B Chapter 3

C Chapter 4

D Chapter 5

7 Where would you look to find the meaning of a word used in the book?

A glossary

B index

C table of contents

D key words

DICTIONARY AND THESAURUS SKILLS

Two other types of reference sources you might use are a dictionary and a thesaurus.

DICTIONARY

A **dictionary** is a reference book that lists words in alphabetical (ABC) order. A dictionary tells you things about words. It shows how to spell and pronounce each word. Then, it tells you what the word means and how to use it correctly in a sentence. It also shows what part of speech the word is (noun, verb, adjective, and so on).

The example below shows how a word appears in a dictionary.

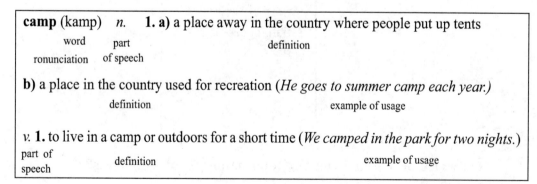

camp (kamp)   *n.*   **1. a)** a place away in the country where people put up tents

　　　word　　　part　　　　　　　　　　　definition
　ronunciation　of speech

b) a place in the country used for recreation (*He goes to summer camp each year.*)

　　　　　　definition　　　　　　　　　　　example of usage

v. **1.** to live in a camp or outdoors for a short time (*We camped in the park for two nights.*)

part of　　　definition　　　　　　　　　　　　example of usage
speech

This dictionary entry shows that *camp* can be used as a noun (*n.*) or a verb (*v.*). You can use this information and the examples of how the word is used to correct and improve your writing.

Read the dictionary entry for *camp*. Is *camp* used correctly in the following sentence?

Last summer, my brother spent two weeks at an overnight camp.

Camp is used correctly in this sentence. You can tell by reading definition 1b and the part of speech for this definition.

THESAURUS

A **thesaurus** is similar to a dictionary. It is a reference book that gives synonyms and antonyms for words. Synonyms have the same meaning as the word you look up; antonyms have the opposite meaning.

This example shows how a word appears in a thesaurus.

> word: **strong**
>
> part of speech: *adjective*
>
> meaning: powerful
>
> synonyms: able, mighty, muscular, sturdy, thick
>
> antonyms: delicate, feeble, weak

Using this thesaurus entry, you can see which words have the similar and opposite meanings of the word *strong*. Notice that synonyms do not always match exactly in meaning. You need to choose the word that fits best into what you are trying to say. Using a thesaurus can also help you avoid repeating words.

A thesaurus can help you find the exact word you want to use. For example, look at this sentence.

The curtains were made of a strong fabric that did not let in much light.

Is there a word that might fit better that *strong* in this sentence? If you said that *thick* fits better, you are right! It describes the curtains more precisely.

Practice 2:   Dictionary and Thesaurus Skills

1   Which synonym for *ate* fits BEST in the blank?

> He ate his broccoli slowly, but he ____ his dessert.

A   devoured   C   tasted

B   nibbled   D   munched

2   Which word makes the writer's meaning the clearest?

> That dog's ____ sounds like a ghost!

A   barking   C   yipping

B   howling   D   woofing

3   What synonym could replace the underlined to make this sentence more interesting?

> We <u>walked</u> happily to the playground.

A   raced   C   stepped

B   plodded   D   trudged

Use the dictionary entry below to answer question 4.

> **shriek** (shreek) *n.* **1** a sharp, loud cry
>
> *v.* **2** to cry out sharply (*She began to shriek in fear.*)

4   Which sentence uses *shriek* correctly?

A   The baby shrieked sleepily after drinking a bottle.

B   The ducks shrieked happily while munching their corn.

C   The child shrieked fearfully in the haunted house.

D   The girl shrieked sadly as she watched her ice cream melt.

Use the thesaurus entry below to answer question 5.

> word: **depressed**
>
> part of speech: *adjective*
>
> meaning: sad, low in spirits
>
> synonyms: saddened, dismayed
>
> antonyms: cheerful, encouraged

5 **Which sentence uses a synonym for *depressed* correctly?**

   A Cheryl was dismayed about losing the tennis match.

   B Alice felt saddened after winning the soccer game.

   C Ron was saddened to get the new video game he had been wanting.

   D Ethan felt dismayed when his mom made his favorite dessert.

USING SOURCES IN ESSAYS

When a writer uses information from another source, he must give a **citation**. Citing a source means telling certain information to show exactly where the facts came from. There are two main reasons for this. First, this helps a reader to find the source to learn more. Second, this gives the source credit for doing the work or thinking of the idea.

When you read a reference book or a research paper, you will sometimes see this source information. Understanding how to use the source information will help you to find that source to learn more. You might find source information in the bibliography, footnotes, or appendix.

A **bibliography** is a list of sources the writer used in the essay. It is located on a page by itself at the end of the paper. Here is an example of an entry you would see in a bibliography.

Berthon, Simon, and Andrew Robinson. *The Shape of the World*. Chicago:

                author   title   publisher city

Rand McNally, 1991.

publisher   date
   name   published

A **footnote** is a note at the bottom of a page in the essay that gives more information about an idea. A footnote can include some source information. Each footnote has a number, which goes with the same number found in the text. Here is an example of a footnote.

[1]See Berthon and Robinson 47–51.

           author   page

Sometimes a paper or a book will have **end notes** instead of footnotes. They are numbered in the same way. But end notes appear at the end of the paper or book instead of on each page.

An **appendix** is extra information at the end of a paper or a book. Readers who want to learn more about the topic will look here. An appendix can include maps, charts, bibliographies, and other sources of information.

You may also see source information within the essay itself. This information will be brief. You can find full information on the source in the bibliography.

Practice 3: Using Sources in Essays

Read the entry from a bibliography. Use the information to answer questions 1 and 2.

White, E.B. *Charlotte's Web*. New York: Dell, 1952.

1 What is the last name of the author?

A Charlotte B White C Web D Dell

2 In what year was this book published?

A 2002 B 2009 C 1952 D 1852

3 Julio is reading a research paper about recycling. He sees a source mentioned that looks interesting. Where would he look to find complete information on that source?

A bibliography C appendix

B footnote D in the essay

4 A writer wants to include a section of extra information about his topic for his readers. Where would he put this extra information?

A bibliography C appendix

B footnote D in the essay

5 Where would you look to find a brief note about an idea mentioned in the essay?

A bibliography C appendix

B footnote D in the essay

CHAPTER 8 SUMMARY

When you do **research**, you find out about a topic. You can use many kinds of **sources** to find information, like magazines, books, and the Internet. You can also use **parts of a book** (like a table of contents) to help you find information within the book.

A **dictionary** helps you use and spell words correctly.

A **thesaurus** helps you use words precisely.

You can use source information in an essay to find more information on the topic.

When you write, you need to give **citations** about your sources. Source information can also be found in the **bibliography**, **footnotes** or **end notes**, or the **appendix**.

CHAPTER 8 REVIEW

1   Which source would be BEST for learning which oceans border the United States?

    A   almanac   B   atlas   C   magazine   D   keywords

2   Which source would be BEST for finding out a word that means the same thing as "leap"?

    A   Internet   B   dictionary   C   thesaurus   D   magazine

3   Which source would be BEST for learning about an election in your state?

    A   newspaper   B   magazine   C   dictionary   D   almanac

For questions 4 and 5, use the excerpt from the table of contents below.

Table of Contents
Chapter 1 Mercury..............................3
Chapter 2 Venus................................12
Chapter 3 Earth.................................36
Chapter 4 Mars.................................55

4   On which page does the chapter about Venus begin?

    A   3   B   12   C   36   D   55

5   Which chapter would you look in to find information about Mars?

    A   Chapter 1   B   Chapter 2   C   Chapter 3   D   Chapter 4

6   Which synonym for *put* fits BEST in the blank?

Susie angrily ____ the book on the table after she had been interrupted for the fourth time.

    A   slammed

    B   set

    C   placed

    D   laid

Use the dictionary entry below to answer question 7.

> **close** (klohz) *v.* **1.** to shut a passage (*Close the window, please.*) **2.** to block (*They had to close the road due to the landslide.*)

7 Which sentence uses *close* correctly?

A Did you close your bed this morning?

B Close the scrap paper you dropped on the floor.

C Did Mr. Ryan ask you to close the lights?

D Close the door before bugs get in the house!

8 Which word makes the writer's meaning the clearest?

> The syrup tipped over, making a _____ mess.

A gluey   B sticky   C wet   D runny

Read the entry from a bibliography below. Use the information to answer questions 9 and 10.

> Rowling, J.K. *Harry Potter and the Sorcerer's Stone.* New York: Scholastic, 1997.

9 In what year was the book published?

A 2009

B 1009

C 1997

D 2007

10 In what city was the book published?

A New York

B London

C Los Angeles

D Atlanta

11 Where would you look to find a list of sources a writer had used in an essay?

A appendix

B table of contents

C bibliography

D index

GA 5 CRCT ELA
Practice Test 1

The purpose of this practice test is to evaluate your skills in a variety of areas linked to the grade 5 English Language Arts standards published by the Georgia Department of Education.

This test is set up in two sections, like the actual CRCT. When you take the CRCT, you have forty-five to seventy minutes to complete each section, with a ten-minute break between them.

GENERAL DIRECTIONS

1 **Read all directions carefully.**

2 **Read each selection.**

3 **Read each question or example. Then, choose the best answer.**

4 **Choose only one answer for each question. If you change an answer, be sure to erase the answer completely.**

Section 1

1   **What part of speech is the underlined word in the sentence?**   5C1a

> Briana's sister <u>takes</u> dance lessons; she is very talented.

A   noun

B   verb

C   conjunction

D   interjection

2   **What is the BEST way to combine these sentences?**   5C1b

> Vito has four marbles. There are two red ones. There are two green ones.

A   Vito has four marbles; two red ones, and two green ones.

B   Vito has four marbles: two red ones and two green ones.

C   Vito has four marbles, two red ones, and two green ones.

D   Vito has four marbles: two red ones; two green ones.

3   **Which verb phrase BEST completes the sentence?**   5C1c

> Zane _____ a puppy from the animal shelter yesterday.

A   is rescuing

B   have rescued

C   rescues

D   rescued

4   What kind of sentence is this?   5C1e

> While my mother cooked breakfast, my father read the newspaper.

A   simple

B   compound

C   complex

D   compound-complex

5   The following paragraph is an example of what organizational structure?   5W1c

> Television may be harmful to young children. Just what is so wrong with watching TV? Some children spend too much time in front of the TV screen when they could be outside playing and getting exercise. Also, certain TV shows are inappropriate for younger viewers; some shows have crimes, drugs, or cussing.

A   cause and effect

B   chronological order

C   question and answer

D   compare and contrast

6   Which is the BEST closing sentence for the paragraph above?   5W2

A   It is important for parents to be aware of what their children watch.

B   Kids are smart enough to know what to watch and what not to watch.

C   No child should be allowed to watch television shows.

D   Parents should cut down on their TV watching as well.

7   What part of speech is the underlined word in the sentence?   5C1a

> Mimi <u>and</u> Nadia enjoy scrapbooking.

A   adjective

B   adverb

C   preposition

D   conjunction

8 **Which sentence uses an apostrophe correctly?**   5C1g

   A Luann read's more books than anyone I know!

   B Jane's brother made the varsity baseball team.

   C A caterpillar lives in it's cocoon to become a butterfly.

   D I did'nt know the answer to the math question.

9 **Which is the BEST topic sentence for the paragraph below?**   5W2

> You can play fetch with a dog. You can't do that with a cat. You can also train a dog to do tricks. Cats just stare at you when you want them to do something. Dogs are very loyal too. They will do their best to protect you. If you want a really good pet, get a dog. They are the best kind of pet!

   A A cat can make a very nice pet.

   B Cats and dogs are fun to play with.

   C A dog is a much better pet than a cat.

   D Training a dog to do tricks takes too long.

10 **Which sentence uses *water* as a verb?**   5C1d

   A Will you pour me a glass of water?

   B Helio and Oliva water their plants.

   C Xander went to the new water park yesterday.

   D The Dead Sea is actually filled with salt water.

11 **Which sentence in the paragraph below repeats an idea?**   5W2

> [1]There are lots of neat things to do at the beach. [2]You can swim or make a sandcastle. [3]You can also look for cool shells or dig for clams. [4]There is so much to do when you go to the beach! [5]You can play volleyball too.

   A sentence 2

   B sentence 3

   C sentence 4

   D sentence 5

12 Which verb phrase BEST completes the sentence?   5C1c

> Brice _____ his poem in class tomorrow.

A recite

B will reciting

C recited

D will recite

13 Which of these is a complete sentence?   5C1f

A Ava lives next door.

B In the brick house.

C Stands on top of a hill.

D She and her four sisters.

14 What part of speech is the underlined word in the sentence?   5C1a

> The racecar zoomed <u>around</u> the track in record time.

A adverb

B preposition

C adjective

D interjection

15 Which transition would BEST connect the two sentences?   5W1d

> Susan wanted to play outside. Her mother made her study for her spelling test.

A so

B and

C however

D consequently

16 What type of sentence is this? 5C1e

> Contrary to popular belief, koalas are not actually bears.

A declarative

B imperative

C exclamatory

D interrogative

17 What is the BEST way to correct this sentence? 5C1b

> Running for the bus, my book fell in the mud.

A Running for the bus, the mud was where I dropped my book.

B My book fell in the mud while running for the bus.

C While running for the bus, I dropped my book in the mud.

D Running for the bus, my book was dropped in the mud.

18 The paragraph below is written in which point of view? 5W1a

> Mary Anne went to the store with her mother. She looked at all the food. There was so much to choose from! She picked out five delicious red apples. Her mother was making an apple pie.

A first person

B second person

C third person

D There is no point of view.

19 Which is the BEST way to correct this run-on? 5C1g

> Neddie made a sandwich, it was roast beef.

A Neddie made a sandwich; and it was roast beef.

B Neddie made a sandwich it was roast beef.

C Neddie made a sandwich; it was roast beef.

D Neddie made a sandwich and it was roast beef.

20 What part of speech is the underlined word in the sentence? 5C1a

> Eli made a family tree with all of <u>his</u> relatives.

A adjective

B noun

C verb

D pronoun

21 Which word would BEST replace the underlined word in the sentence? 5W3g

> Holly forgot to <u>examine</u> for her science test.

A report

B survey

C study

D analyze

22 The following paragraph is an example of what organizational structure? 5W1c

> Ray and Bobby might be brothers, but they are very different people. Ray is older than Bobby by four years. Bobby has red hair and freckles just like his mom, and Ray has his dad's dark hair and green eyes. They both like to play sports, but they enjoy different ones. Ray plays soccer, and Bobby plays baseball. They may be different, but at least they get along.

A cause and effect

B compare and contrast

C question and answer

D chronological order

23 Which word would BEST complete this sentence? 5C1g

> You can't eat in here; it is not _____.

A alowed

B aloud

C allowed

D alloud

24 **Which transition would BEST connect the two sentences?**   5W1d

> Chris ate all of his vegetables. His mother let him have dessert.

A so

B although

C but

D since

25 **What type of sentence is this?**   5C1e

> When is your sister's birthday?

A declarative

B imperative

C exclamatory

D interrogative

26 **What is the BEST way to combine these sentences?**   5C1b

> Michele wants to be an astronaut when she grows up. She could also be the president.

A Michele wants to be an astronaut when she grows up, and she also could be the president.

B Michele wants to be an astronaut when she grows up and also the president.

C Michele wants to be either an astronaut or the president when she grows up.

D Michele wants to be an astronaut when she grows up; or also could be the president.

27 Which sentence in the paragraph below does not belong and should be removed?

5W2

> [1]There have been many Batman movies. [2]In every movie, Batman fights a new villain. [3]The most recent Batman movie made was *The Dark Knight*. [4]Heath Ledger played Batman's enemy, the Joker. [5]Jack Nicholson has played the Joker before. [6]*The Dark Knight* was a very intense movie.

A sentence 1

B sentence 3

C sentence 5

D sentence 6

28 Which supporting detail is MOST important to add to the paragraph above?

5W2

A Your parents probably won't allow you to see that movie.

B Christian Bale played Batman in *The Dark Knight*.

C Many people saw *The Dark Knight* in movie theatres.

D Jack Nicholson has been in many other movies.

29 Which verb phrase BEST completes the sentence?

5C1c

> John _____ a total of twelve books so far this summer.

A has reading

B have read

C has read

D has readed

30 Which word would BEST replace the underlined word in the sentence?

5W4b

> The ballerina's movements were very <u>fragile</u>.

A delicate

B weak

C frail

D flimsy

Section 2

31 Which is the BEST topic sentence for the paragraph below?   5W2

> The javelin is not a very heavy object, but throwing it long distances requires great arm and leg strength. Training involves many hours of lifting weights and running sprints. Without this preparation, performance will drop and injuries are more of a risk.

A Like the other athletes you see at the Olympics, javelin throwers deserve respect.

B Javelin throwing may look easy on TV, but in reality, it is a very demanding sport.

C I enjoy watching the Olympics, and javelin throwing is my favorite event to watch.

D I bet it is harder to throw a shot put than to toss a javelin a long distance.

32 What part of speech is the underlined word in the sentence?   5C1a

> Don't even think about leaving before <u>you</u> clean your room!

A verb

B conjunction

C pronoun

D preposition

33 Which word would BEST complete this sentence?   5C1g

> The magician was a master of _____.

A omission

B allusion

C emission

D illusion

34 Which sentence uses a comma correctly?   5C1g

A Helen wanted to raise money to find a cure for cancer, but she could not think of a fundraiser.

B Helen wanted to raise money to find a cure, for cancer, but she could not think of a fundraiser.

C Helen wanted to raise money, to find a cure for cancer but she could not think of a fundraiser.

D Helen wanted to raise money to find a cure for cancer but she could not, think of a fundraiser.

35 Which transition would BEST connect the two sentences?   5W1d

> Manny did not finish his chores. That meant he could not play outside.

A fortunately

B unfortunately

C meanwhile

D although

36 What part of speech is the underlined word in the sentence?   5C1a

> *Monsters, Inc.* is my <u>favorite</u> Disney Pixar movie.

A noun

B verb

C adjective

D adverb

37 This paragraph is an example of what organizational structure?   5W1c

> Researchers have proved that smoking is bad for your health. The American Medical Association has issued several warnings about the increased risk of lung cancer linked with smoking. In addition, the *New England Journal of Medicine* has issued its own separate findings verifying this same link between smoking and lung cancer.

A cause and effect

B chronological order

C question and answer

D compare and contrast

38 Which verb phrase BEST completes the sentence?   5C1c

> Rachelle _____ since she was five years old.

A dancing

B has dancing

C has danced

D will dance

39 Which sentence has the correct punctuation?   5C1f

A I have never been to a music concert, before.

B I want to see: Rhianna perform in person.

C I hear she is a nice person, and she is very pretty.

D Maybe my mom will buy tickets, my birthday is soon.

40 What kind of sentence is this?   5C1e

> My brother always orders the same thing when we go out to eat.

A simple   C compound

B complex   D compound-complex

41 What part of speech is the underlined word in this sentence?   5C1a

> The band recovered <u>quickly</u> when the singer forgot her cue.

A verb   C noun

B adverb   D pronoun

42 Which sentence in the paragraph below should be removed?   5W2

> [1]It is easier than ever to learn a new language. [2]Soon, you will be able to learn a language by taking an elective course in middle school. [3]Then, if you go to college you may have the opportunity to live in a foreign country as an exchange student. [4]You could even learn martial arts if you wanted. [5]All along the way, you can join chatrooms on the Internet or conversation meetings in your area that will help you practice speaking your new language.

A sentence 1   C sentence 4

B sentence 3   D sentence 5

43 Which sentence from the paragraph above is written in third-person point of view?

A Then, if you go to college you may have the opportunity to live in a foreign country as an exchange student.

B It is easier than ever to learn a new language.

C You could even learn martial arts if you wanted.

D Soon, you will be able to learn a language by taking an elective course in middle school.

44 Which transition would BEST connect the ideas in this sentence?   5W1d

> Remember when we went to the circus _____ we saw the lion tamers and clowns?

A and

B yet

C because

D although

45 Which of these sentences is a fragment?   5C1f

A Brazil is a very large country.

B It is located in South America.

C Very beautiful land and people.

D I would like to travel there one day.

46 What part of speech is the underlined word in the sentence?   5C1a

> Mike jumped down the hall, <u>on</u> the bed, and across the floor.

A verb

B adverb

C noun

D preposition

47 The following paragraph is an example of what organizational structure?   5W1c

> Chet relit the kerosene lantern, bathing the cavern with light. Jagged stalactites covered the cave's ceiling. Bats were flying and squeaking through the cavern. The cave was a fearsome sight.

A narrative

B compare and contrast

C question and answer

D persuasive

48 **If Chet wanted to learn more about how stalactites are formed, what would be the BEST source for him to look at?** 5W3c

A   an article about mineral formations

B   an Internet site about caving safety

C   a map of caves in Georgia

D   a book about Mammoth Cave

49 **Which sentence below is written in first-person point of view?** 5W2

A   He didn't know what she meant.

B   She whispered, "I have a secret."

C   Mom told us all to go outside.

D   They decided to go home then.

50 **What is the BEST way to correct this sentence?** 5C1b

> She left the room fuming.

A   The room was fuming when she left it.

B   Leaving the room fuming, she left.

C   Fuming, she left the room.

D   She left the fuming room.

51 **What kind of sentence is this?** 5C1e

> Benjamin left his trash for someone else to pick up.

A   simple

B   compound

C   complex

D   compound-complex

52 Which sentence in the paragraph below repeats an idea? 5W2

> [1]Nothing can make or break my day more than my attitude. [2]It is more important than what I'm wearing, what I'm going to eat for lunch, or how my hair turned out. [3]My attitude is important to making my day good or bad. [4]I've learned when I smile at people, they smile back. [5]Concentrating on being positive can turn my day around.

   A   sentence 2

   B   sentence 3

   C   sentence 4

   D   sentence 5

53 Which supporting detail is MOST important to add to the paragraph above? 5W2

   A   When I'm touchy or grouchy, people back away from me.

   B   Sandy on *SpongeBob SquarePants* has a happy attitude.

   C   Rap stars often express bad attitudes.

   D   Statistics have proved that a bad attitude can get you fired.

54 Which word would BEST replace the underlined word in the sentence? 5W4b

> Mark's grade on the exam was <u>boring</u>.

   A   ineffective

   B   unpleasant

   C   disappointing

   D   bitter

55 Which sentence uses *practice* as an adjective? 5C1d

   A   Meet on the practice field at 3 p.m.

   B   We have to practice our songs tonight.

   C   Do we have football practice tomorrow?

   D   Neil makes a point to practice his guitar daily.

56 Which sentence uses the correct words?   5C1g

   A   The sad song effected Cameron deeply.

   B   The pitcher frame broke when it fell off the desk.

   C   I don't no if I can go to the park with you.

   D   Millie looks all grown up in her new dress.

57 Which verb phrase BEST completes the sentence?   5C1c

> Oliver's mom wanted to get to Ohio quickly, so she _____ all night.

   A   has driven

   B   drove

   C   is driving

   D   drives

58 Which of these is a run-on?   5C1f

   A   Milo likes airplanes; Rodney likes trains.

   B   Emilia wants to buy a puppy and a kitten.

   C   Wendy went to the store, she bought milk.

   D   Billy hit the ball, and then he ran to first base.

59 What part of speech is the underlined word in the sentence?   5C1a

> Cory does not like to ride the school <u>bus</u>.

   A   noun

   B   pronoun

   C   preposition

   D   verb

60 What is the BEST way to combine these sentences?   5C1b

> The movie was boring. We sat through the whole thing.

   A   The movie was boring, so we sat through the whole thing.

   B   Even though the movie was boring, we sat through the whole thing.

   C   We sat through the whole movie, and it was boring.

   D   Because the movie was so boring, we sat through the whole thing.

GA 5 CRCT ELA
Practice Test 2

The purpose of this practice test is to evaluate your skills in a variety of areas linked to the grade 5 English Language Arts standards published by the Georgia Department of Education.

This test is set up in two sections, like the actual CRCT. When you take the CRCT, you have forty-five to seventy minutes to complete each section, with a ten-minute break between them.

GENERAL DIRECTIONS

1 **Read all directions carefully.**

2 **Read each selection.**

3 **Read each question or example. Then, choose the best answer.**

4 **Choose only one answer for each question. If you change an answer, be sure to erase the answer completely.**

Section 1

1 **The following paragraph is an example of what organizational structure?** 5W1c

> I really hate Brussels sprouts. Why do I hate them so much? They are one of the most disgusting vegetables imaginable. The little green ball-shaped vegetables look like eyeballs staring at me. I also dislike the taste. My mom calls it a "delicate, nutty flavor." I call it just plain gross. I cannot even stand the smell! They smell like sulfur! Even if I liked the way they looked and tasted, I could not get past the smell.

A cause and effect

B chronological order

C question and answer

D compare and contrast

2 **Which is the BEST closing sentence for the paragraph above?** 5W2

A Brussels sprouts are a healthy vegetable.

B Brussels sprouts are just not for me.

C My sister enjoys Brussels sprouts.

D I wish I liked Brussels sprouts.

3 **What part of speech is the underlined word in the sentence?** 5C1a

> Macy easily made friends with the new girl at school.

A noun

B conjunction

C interjection

D adverb

4 **What kind of sentence is this?** 5C1e

> Ina Garten has a cooking show on the Food Network.

A simple

B compound

C complex

D compound-complex

5 **Which verb phrase BEST completes the sentence?** 5C1c

> Is there anyone who _____ to take out the trash tomorrow?

A volunteering

B would volunteered

C will volunteer

D has been volunteering

6 **What is the BEST way to combine these sentences?** 5C1b

> Louie enjoys learning about science. He likes to understand the solar system. He likes to observe plant life.

A Louie enjoys learning about science; he likes to understand the solar system, and he likes to observe plant life.

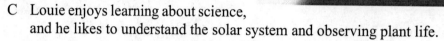

B Louie enjoys learning about science, especially understanding the solar system and observing plant life.

C Louie enjoys learning about science, and he likes to understand the solar system and observing plant life.

D Louie enjoys learning about science; he likes to understand the solar system; he likes to observe plant life.

7 **Which sentence uses *toy* as an adjective?** 5C1d

A Is that your toy dog on the shelf?

B Dad bought me a new toy today.

C Don't toy with your food, Robert.

D There is a big toy underneath the tree.

8 **Which is the BEST topic sentence for the paragraph below?** 5W2

> Each family tries to bring in the best entree or dessert. Mrs. Reid's chicken spaghetti is very tasty. It is a fierce challenge to Mr. Ewing's homemade barbecue. Laramie brings in two delectable apple pies. They are sure to be gone in seconds. Everyone loves Miss Hooper's homemade ice cream. This potluck dinner is deliciously serious business.

A I love to eat at the church potluck dinner.

B Our church always has lots of food at potluck dinners.

C At the church potluck dinner, there is always a competition.

D It's hard to leave hungry when you eat at the potluck dinner.

9 **Which sentence uses a comma correctly?** 5C1g

A Aaron wondered, why they had not left for the restaurant yet.

B We'll probably be home in time to watch, the game, right?

C Christopher Columbus, the famous sailor sailed, in 1492.

D For Dana's birthday, I think we should get her *Rock Band*.

10 **What part of speech is the underlined word in the sentence?**   5C1a

| Freddie's favorite sweater is the <u>navy</u> blue one. |

A adjective

B pronoun

C interjection

D conjunction

11 **Which sentence in the paragraph below repeats an idea?**   5W2

[1]Harry Houdini was a magician. [2]He did magic tricks and risky stunts. [3]He would tie himself up and hang upside down from a crane. [4]Minutes later, he would escape. [5]He always came up with crazy stunts to do. [6]Sometimes he would tie his hands and go into a glass box. [7]The box would be locked and filled with water while he was in it. [8]Seconds later, he would come out, alive and well.

A sentence 4

B sentence 5

C sentence 6

D sentence 7

12 **If someone wanted to look up more information about Harry Houdini, what would be the BEST source to use?**   5W3b

A a book of magic tricks

B a biography about Houdini

C an article about breathing under water

D a magazine article about optical illusions

13 **Which transition would BEST connect the two sentences?**   5W1d

| Jill is trying to teach her sister the alphabet. Jamie can't even talk. |

A consequently

B fortunately

C and so

D even though

14 What type of sentence is this?   5C1e

> Please finish your tests and bring them to me.

A interrogative   C imperative

B declarative   D exclamatory

15 What part of speech is the underlined word in the sentence?   5C1a

> They got there just after the <u>movie</u> started.

A noun

B verb

C pronoun

D adverb

16 Which of these is a sentence fragment?   5C1f

A Cole wants to play the tuba.

B He is going to be in the school band.

C Not too many tuba players in fifth grade.

D He has a good chance of getting a spot.

17 Which is the BEST way to correct this run-on?   5C1g

> My aunt bought a new purse yesterday it is an original Coach bag.

A My aunt bought a new purse yesterday, it is an original Coach bag.

B My aunt bought a new purse yesterday and it is an original Coach bag.

C My aunt bought a new purse yesterday; and it is an original Coach bag.

D My aunt bought a new purse yesterday; it is an original Coach bag.

18 What part of speech is the underlined word in the sentence?   5C1a

> Haaj decided to run <u>for</u> class president next year.

A adjective

B preposition

C pronoun

D interjection

19 **Which word would BEST replace the underlined word in the sentence?** 5W3g

> Grandma's chocolate cake is the most <u>appetizing</u> dessert.

A delicious

B inviting

C agreeable

D attractive

20 **Which sentence is written in first-person point of view?** 5W1a

A I have to tell you about our trip to the circus!

B There were elephants, clowns, and lion tamers.

C The master of ceremonies introduced each act.

D It was a perfect way to spend a Saturday afternoon.

21 **What is the BEST way to correct this sentence?** 5C1b

> Every Friday, the cafeteria serves pizza to students on paper plates.

A The cafeteria serves pizza to students on paper plates every Friday.

B Every Friday, the cafeteria serves pizza on paper plates to students.

C Every Friday, the cafeteria, on paper plates, serves pizza to students.

D The cafeteria serves every Friday pizza to students on paper plates.

22 **Which word would BEST complete this sentence?** 5C1g

> That flower has pretty, colorful _____.

A petals

B pedals

C peddles

D pettles

23 **What type of sentence is this?** 5C1e

> Will you take me to the game tomorrow?

A declarative

B imperative

C exclamatory

D interrogative

24 Which transition would BEST connect the two sentences?   5W1d

> To get the project done in time, Toby typed up the report, _____ Nina decorated the poster.

A for

B so

C however

D while

25 The following paragraph is an example of what organizational structure?   5W1c

> The two great locomotives stood head to head on the tracks. Hundreds of people gathered around to witness the historic event. For the first time, a railroad line had been completed that joined East and West. The scene was Promontory Summit, Utah Territory, in 1869.

A persuasive

B narrative

C compare and contrast

D question and answer

26 What is the BEST way to expand this sentence to give more detail?   5C1b

> I left my watch on the desk at my grandma's house.

A I left my new watch on the desk at my grandma's house last week.

B I left my new watch on the desk at Grandma Ruth's house.

C I left my brand-new watch on the desk at Grandma Ruth's house when I visited last week.

D I left my watch on the desk at my grandma's house when I went over there.

27 Which sentence in the paragraph below does not belong and should be removed?   5W2

> [1]People don't give weightlifters enough credit. [2]Lifting weights is both mentally and physically demanding. [3]The lifter knows that form is crucial. [4]The lifter must visualize what he or she is doing during every second of a lift. [5]People who do not exercise their minds in this manner end up with strains, sprains, and back and neck injuries.

A sentence 1

B sentence 2

C sentence 3

D sentence 4

28 Which supporting detail is MOST important to add to the paragraph above?   5W2

A Most weightlifters are men, but some women lift weights too.

B Weights are really heavy, so be careful when you try to lift them.

C A standard weight bar is around seven feet long and forty-four pounds.

D It takes a great amount of concentration to lift large weights safely.

29 Which verb BEST completes the sentence?   5C1c

> I don't mind _____ math tests because I am great at math.

A takes

B taking

C took

D taken

30 Which of these sentences is a run-on?   5C1f

A When you come over, we can play video games.

B My cousin's birthday is tomorrow, but mine is Tuesday.

C Brock has four sisters, he is the youngest in the family.

D Michella's family owns a farm, and she feeds the chickens.

Section 2

31 **What part of speech is the underlined word in the sentence?** 5C1a

> We saw tigers, penguins, <u>and</u> pandas at the zoo.

A adverb

B pronoun

C conjunction

D interjection

32 **Which transition would BEST connect the two sentences?** 5W1d

> Evan's parents gave him money for his birthday. He spent it on a new iPod.

A but

B so

C when

D while

33 **Which is the BEST topic sentence for the paragraph below?** 5W2

> Though they were first built in Egypt, aqueducts have come to be associated with Rome. This is due to the Romans' great engineering, which was among the most skilled in the world. The Romans used huge stone arches to support the channels. Some of these sloping waterways were dozens of miles long. Though these systems were well built, most of them fell apart years later because of poor maintenance. However, a few are still being used to distribute water in Spain to this day.

A The Aztecs and Harappans built aqueduct systems of their own.

B Romans weren't first to use aqueducts, but they greatly improved the design of these systems.

C Rome's enemies used the aqueducts to poison Rome's water from miles away.

D The aqueduct is perhaps the greatest invention in human history.

34 **Which word would BEST complete this sentence?**   5C1g

Lina _____ the present and added a beautiful bow.

A wrapped

B wrapt

C rapt

D rapped

35 **What part of speech is the underlined word in the sentence?**   5C1a

<u>Ow</u>! I stubbed my toe!

A adjective

B conjunction

C preposition

D interjection

36 **Which sentence uses commas correctly?**   5C1g

   A "Sheila please come to the front office," said the voice on the intercom.

   B "Sheila please come to the front office" said the voice on the intercom.

   C "Sheila, please come to the front office," said the voice on the intercom.

   D "Sheila, please come, to the front office," said the voice on the intercom.

37 **This paragraph is an example of what organizational structure?**   5W1c

My two favorite fruits are apples and oranges. Both fruits are very nutritious snacks. There are many kinds of apples; some are red, and some are green. Depending on the type, the apple might be sweet or tart. Also, apples don't have to be peeled to be eaten. Oranges are usually the color of their name: orange. They have a citrusy flavor, because they are rich in vitamin C. An orange needs to be peeled to be eaten properly. But, both fruits can be juiced to make a refreshing drink.

A compare and contrast

B question and answer

C chronological order

D cause and effect

38 **What part of speech is the underlined word in this sentence?**   5C1a

Nell <u>learned</u> to juggle, and she's gotten very good at it.

A verb

B adverb

C noun

D pronoun

39 **What kind of sentence is this?**   5C1e

East and West Berlin used to be separated by the Berlin Wall, but it was finally torn down in 1989.

A simple

B complex

C compound

D compound-complex

40 **Which sentence has the correct punctuation?**   5C1f

A Does anyone know what time it is.

B I can't seem to find: my watch.

C If anyone sees it, please let me know.

D I might have to get a new one; if I can't find it.

41 **Which verb phrase BEST completes the sentence?**   5C1c

Paul's big brother _____ football for four years.

A playing

B has playing

C has played

D will play

42 Which transition would BEST connect the ideas in this sentence?   5W1d

> Dad got tickets to a Georgia Tech football game _____ I had never been to a college game before.

A because

B although

C and

D yet

43 What part of speech is the underlined word in the sentence?   5C1a

> Marci had to catch the school bus so <u>she</u> wouldn't be late.

A noun

B verb

C adverb

D pronoun

44 Which of these sentences is a fragment?   5C1f

A Yodeling is an interesting form of singing.

B Probably was developed in the Alpine region.

C Yodelers sing long notes ranging in pitch.

D It takes much practice to perfect a yodel.

45 Which sentence in the paragraph below should be removed? 5W2

> ¹It is really easy to make a puppet. ²All you need is a sock, markers, glue, and buttons. ³Place the sock on your hand, and use your fingers and thumb to move the sock up and down like a mouth. ⁴Draw lips on your puppet, and glue buttons for eyes. ⁵Pom-poms are a fun craft to make too. ⁶You can decorate it however you want. ⁷You can add ears, clothes, or even a hat. ⁸It's a fun craft for you and your friends to do together.

A   sentence 1

B   sentence 4

C   sentence 5

D   sentence 7

46 What sentence from the paragraph above is written in second-person point of view? 5W2

A   It is really easy to make a puppet.

B   You can add ears, clothes, or even a hat.

C   Draw lips on your puppet, and glue buttons for eyes.

D   Pom-poms are a fun craft to make too.

47 What kind of sentence is this? 5C1e

> Before you go outside, please put on your coat.

A   simple

B   complex

C   compound

D   compound-complex

48 The sentence below is written in what point of view? 5W2

> I can't believe I met Nick Jonas!

A   first person

B   second person

C   third person

D   It does not have a point of view.

49 What is the BEST way to correct this sentence?   5C1b

> After dropping his tennis racket, Bill's elbow was injured.

A After dropping his tennis racket, Bill injured his elbow.

B Bill's elbow was injured after dropping his tennis racket.

C After his tennis racket dropped, Bill's elbow was injured.

D After his tennis racket was dropping, Bill injured his elbow.

50 Which verb phrase BEST completes the sentence?   5C1c

> Melanie _____ for the school play tomorrow.

A auditioned

B will audition

C was auditioning

D has auditioned

51 The following paragraph is an example of what organizational structure? 5W1c

> Kyle had the best birthday party yesterday. He had five friends over to his house. They played video games and shot hoops in the driveway. Kyle's mom made hamburgers and hotdogs. They ate so much food, and still had room left for cake and ice cream. It was a great day.

A cause and effect   C question and answer

B chronological order   D compare and contrast

52 Which verb phrase BEST completes the sentence?   5C1c

> Yolanda _____ a solo in church yesterday.

A has sung   C is singing

B sang   D sings

53 Which word would BEST replace the underlined word in the sentence? 5W4b

> Utilize the hammer to embed the nail in the wood.

A swing   C operate

B employ   D handle

54 **Which sentence uses the correct underlined word?**   5C1g

    A Your performance <u>revue</u> is coming up next week.

    B The bride looked beautiful walking down the <u>aisle</u>.

    C Vicky promised she was a skilled <u>righter</u>.

    D Lucas gave Bree a red <u>rows</u> for her birthday.

55 **Which sentence in the paragraph below repeats an idea?**   5W2

> [1]Grant stopped running through the sand for a moment to check his progress. [2]He could hear the crashing of the waves. [3]Squawking sea gulls circled above him. [4]The waves were noisy as they lapped up the shore. [5]The smell of salt water hung thick in the air.

    A sentence 1

    B sentence 3

    C sentence 4

    D sentence 5

56 **Which closing sentence would be the BEST for the paragraph above?**   5W2

    A Grant realized he had finally reached the ocean.

    B The sea is very different from the mountains.

    C Then, a jellyfish came ashore and stung him.

    D Grant was training for a marathon.

57 **Which sentence uses *bow* as a noun?**   5C1d

    A After you dance, don't forget to bow.

    B Did you put a big bow on the present?

    C Richie had to bow before the Queen.

    D Can you bow properly, or should I show you?

58 **What part of speech is the underlined word in the sentence?**   5C1a

> Sally likes to study about <u>exotic</u> birds.

    A noun

    B pronoun

    C adjective

    D adverb

59 **Which word would BEST replace the underlined word in the sentence?**   5W4b

> She made an exquisite turn and then <u>lurched</u> gracefully into the air.

A galloped

B wobbled

C hopped

D leaped

60 Which of these sentences is a run-on?   5C1f

A Elsie has a sister who is in high school.

B Ron got strep throat last week and missed school.

C Connie's mom is really nice she bakes cookies.

D Bradley passes and catches the football like a pro.

American Book Company

The Standards Experts

MASTERING THE

GEORGIA 5TH GRADE CRCT

IN

ENGLISH LANGUAGE ARTS

Answer Key

February 2010

American Book Company
PO Box 2638
Woodstock, GA 30188-1383
Toll Free: 1 (888) 264-5877   Phone: (770) 928-2834
Fax: (770) 928-7483   Toll Free Fax: 1 (866) 827-3240
www.americanbookcompany.com

GEORGIA 5TH GRADE CRCT IN ENGLISH LANGUAGE ARTS

Chart of Standards

The following chart correlates each question on the Diagnostic Test, Practice Test 1, and Practice Test 2 to the reading standards and associated concepts, skills, and abilities published by the Georgia Department of Education. These test questions are also correlated with chapters in *Mastering the Georgia 5th Grade CRCT in English Language Arts*.

Concepts, Skills, and Abilities	Diagnostic Test	Practice Test 1	Practice Test 2	Chapter	CCS Addressed
Domain: Research/Writing Process					
Research and Writing Process refers to students' skill in using and analyzing the purpose of research and technology, using resources to support the writing process, and evaluating the various strategies, styles, and purposes of written organization.					
ELA5W1 The student produces writing that establishes an appropriate organizational structure, sets a context and engages the reader, maintains a coherent focus throughout, and signals a satisfying closure. The student					
a. Selects a focus, an organizational structure, and a point of view based on purpose, genre expectations, audience, length, and format requirements.					
	37	18	20	6	Writing 1.a, 2.a, 3.a, 4
b. Writes texts of a length appropriate to address the topic or tell the story.					
	n/a	n/a	n/a	7	Writing 4
c. Uses traditional structures for conveying information (e.g., chronological order, cause and effect, similarity and difference, and posing and answering a question).					
	8, 23, 48	5, 22, 37, 47	1, 25, 37, 51	6	Writing 1.a, 2.a, 3.a, 4
d. Uses appropriate structures to ensure coherence (e.g., transition elements).					
	18, 24, 35, 47	15, 24, 35, 44	13, 24, 32, 42	6	Writing 1.c, 2.c, 3.c, 4

Concepts, Skills, & Abilities	Diagnostic Test	Practice Test 1	Practice Test 2	Chapter	CCS Addressed

ELA5W2 The student demonstrates competence in a variety of genres.

The student produces a narrative that:

a. Engages the reader by establishing a context, creating a point of view, and otherwise developing reader interest.

b. Establishes a plot, point of view, setting, and conflict, and/or the significance of events.

c. Creates an organizing structure.

d. Includes sensory details and concrete language to develop plot and character.

e. Excludes extraneous details and inconsistencies.

f. Develops complex characters through actions describing the motivation of characters and character conversation.

g. Uses a range of appropriate narrative strategies such as flashback, foreshadowing, dialogue, tension, or suspense.

h. Provides a sense of closure to the writing.

i. Lifts the level of language using appropriate strategies including word choice.

The student produces informational writing (e.g., report, procedures, correspondence) that:

a. Engages the reader by establishing a context, creating a speaker's voice, and otherwise developing reader interest.

b. Develops a controlling idea that conveys a perspective on a subject.

c. Creates an organizing structure appropriate to a specific purpose, audience, and context.

d. Includes appropriate facts and details.

e. Excludes extraneous details and inappropriate information.

f. Uses a range of appropriate strategies, such as providing facts and details, describing or analyzing the subject, and narrating a relevant anecdote.

g. Draws from more than one source of information such as speakers, books, newspapers, and online materials.

h. Provides a sense of closure to the writing.

i. Lifts the level of language using appropriate strategies including word choice.

The student produces a response to literature that:

a. Engages the reader by establishing a context, creating a speaker's voice, and otherwise developing reader interest.

b. Advances a judgment that is interpretive, evaluative, or reflective.

c. Supports judgments through references to the text, other works, authors, or non-print media, or references to personal knowledge.

d. Develops interpretations that exhibit careful reading and demonstrate an understanding of the literary work.

e. Excludes extraneous details and inappropriate information.

f. Provides a sense of closure to the writing.

g. Lifts the level of language using appropriate strategies including word choice.

Concepts, Skills, & Abilities	Diagnostic Test	Practice Test 1	Practice Test 2	Chapter	CCS Addressed

The student produces a persuasive essay that:

a. Engages the reader by establishing a context, creating a speaker's voice, and otherwise developing reader interest.

b. States a clear position in support of a proposal.

c. Supports a position with relevant evidence.

d. Creates an organizing structure appropriate to a specific purpose, audience, and context.

e. Addresses reader concerns.

f. Excludes extraneous details and inappropriate information.

g. Provides a sense of closure to the writing.

h. Raises the level of language using appropriate strategies (word choice).

	Diagnostic Test	Practice Test 1	Practice Test 2	Chapter	CCS Addressed
	13, 14, 19, 27, 28, 36, 42, 43, 52, 53, 60	6, 9, 11, 27, 28, 31, 42, 43, 49, 52, 53	2, 8, 11, 27, 28, 33, 45, 46, 48, 55, 56	6, 7	Writing 1.a–d, 2.a–b, 2.d–e, 3.a–e, 4, 5, 7, 8, 9.a–b Language 3.a, 6 Reading Info 7, 9 Reading Lit 10

ELA5W3 The student uses research and technology to support writing. The student

a. Acknowledges information from sources.

b. Uses organizational features of printed text (i.e., citations, end notes, bibliographic references, appendices) to locate relevant information.

c. Uses various reference materials (i.e., dictionary, thesaurus, encyclopedia, electronic information, almanac, atlas, magazines, newspapers) as aids to writing.

	Diagnostic Test	Practice Test 1	Practice Test 2	Chapter	CCS Addressed
	9, 49	48	12	7, 8	Writing 7, 8, 9 Reading Info 7, 9 Language 2.e, 4.c

d. Uses the features of texts (e.g., index, table of contents, guide words, alphabetical/ numerical order) to obtain and organize information and thoughts.

e. Demonstrates basic keyboarding skills and familiarity with computer terminology (e.g., software, memory, disk drive, hard drive).

f. Creates simple documents by using electronic media and employing organizational features (e.g., passwords, entry and pull-down menus, word searches, thesaurus, spell check).

g. Uses a thesaurus to identify alternative word choices and meanings.

	Diagnostic Test	Practice Test 1	Practice Test 2	Chapter	CCS Addressed
	22	21	19	7, 8	Writing 6 Language 2.e, 4.c

ELA5W4 The student consistently uses a writing process to develop, revise, and evaluate writing. The student

a. Plans and drafts independently and resourcefully.

	Diagnostic Test	Practice Test 1	Practice Test 2	Chapter	CCS Addressed
	n/a	n/a	n/a	7	Writing 1.a, 2.a, 3.a, 4, 10

b. Revises manuscripts to improve the meaning and focus of writing by adding, deleting, consolidating, clarifying, and rearranging words and sentences.

	Diagnostic Test	Practice Test 1	Practice Test 2	Chapter	CCS Addressed
	29, 54	30, 54	53, 59	6, 7, 8	Writing 1.b, 2.b, 2.d, 3.c, 3.d, 5 Language 3.a

c. Edits to correct errors in spelling, punctuation, etc.

	Diagnostic Test	Practice Test 1	Practice Test 2	Chapter	CCS Addressed
	n/a	n/a	n/a	7	Writing 5 Language 1, 2.a–e

Concepts, Skills, & Abilities	Diagnostic Test	Practice Test 1	Practice Test 2	Chapter	CCS Addressed
Domain: Grammar/Sentence Construction					
Grammar and Sentence Construction refers to students' skill in recognizing and applying standard rules of capitalization, punctuation, language usage, and correct standard spelling. This domain also refers to students' achievement in identifying and analyzing various sentence patterns, problematic sentences including sentence fragments and run-ons, and the basic parts of a sentence.					
ELA5C1 The student demonstrates understanding and control of the rules of the English language, realizing that usage involves the appropriate application of conventions and grammar in both written and spoken formats. The student					
a. Uses and identifies the eight parts of speech (e.g., noun, pronoun, verb, adverb, adjective, conjunction, preposition, interjection).					
	1, 3, 7, 20, 31, 33, 40, 50, 59	1, 7, 14, 20, 32, 36, 41, 46, 59	3, 10, 15, 18, 31, 35, 38, 43, 58	1	Language 1.a, 1.e
b. Expands or reduces sentences (e.g., adding or deleting modifiers, combining or revising sentences).					
	4, 17, 30, 32, 45, 55	2, 17, 26, 50, 60	6, 21, 26, 49	5, 6	Languag 3.a
c. Uses and identifies verb phrases and verb tenses.					
	5, 11, 25, 38, 57	3, 12, 29, 38, 57	5, 29, 41, 50, 52	2, 6	Language 1.b–d
d. Recognizes that a word performs different functions according to its position in the sentence.					
	10	10, 55	7, 57	1	Language 1.a
e. Varies the sentence structure by kind (declarative, interrogative, imperative, and exclamatory sentences and functional fragments), order, and complexity (simple, compound, complex, and compound-complex).					
	2, 15, 26, 41, 51	4, 16, 25, 40, 51	4, 14, 23, 39, 47	5, 6	–
f. Uses and identifies correct mechanics (e.g., apostrophes, quotation marks, comma use in compound sentences, paragraph indentations) and correct sentence structure (e.g., elimination of sentence fragments and run-ons).					
	6, 16, 34, 46, 58	13, 39, 45, 58	16, 30, 40, 44, 60	3, 5	Language 1, 2.a–e, 3.a Writing 5
g. Uses additional knowledge of correct mechanics (e.g., apostrophes, quotation marks, comma use in compound sentences, paragraph indentations), correct sentence structure (e.g., elimination of fragments and run-ons), and correct Standard English spelling (e.g., commonly used homophones) when writing, revising, and editing.					
	12, 21, 39, 44, 56	8, 19, 23, 33, 34, 56	9, 17, 22, 34, 36, 54	2, 3, 4, 5	Language 1, 2.a–d, 3 Writing 5

NOT COVERED
Language 3.b

DIAGNOSTIC TEST
Pages 3–20

1. B	11. D	21. B	31. C	41. B	51. B
2. C	12. B	22. A	32. A	42. D	52. B
3. A	13. C	23. D	33. D	43. A	53. C
4. B	14. B	24. B	34. B	44. B	54. A
5. D	15. C	25. C	35. B	45. A	55. B
6. A	16. B	26. B	36. A	46. C	56. C
7. C	17. D	27. A	37. C	47. C	57. A
8. D	18. C	28. B	38. B	48. B	58. D
9. A	19. A	29. D	39. D	49. D	59. B
10. C	20. C	30. C	40. C	50. C	60. B

CHAPTER 1: PARTS OF SPEECH
Practice 1: Nouns and Pronouns
Pages 22–23
1. B   2. D   3. A   4. C   5. A

Practice 2: Verbs
Pages 24–25 (top)
1. D   2. C   3. B   4. B   5. A

Practice 3: Adjectives and Adverbs
Pages 25 (bottom)–26
1. A   2. D   3. A   4. A   5. B

Practice 4: Preposition, Conjunctions, and Interjections
Page 28
1. C   2. A   3. A   4. C   5. D

Chapter 1 Review
Pages 29–30
1. A   2. C   3. A   4. C   5. B   6. D   7. A   8. B   9. B   10. C

CHAPTER 2: USAGE AND GRAMMAR
Practice 1: Verbs
Page 34
1. B   2. A   3. C   4. B   5. D   6. C

Practice 2: Nonstandard English
Pages 36–37
1. B   2. D   3. B   4. D   5. D

Chapter 2 Review
Pages 37–38
1. D   2. C   3. B   4. C   5. D   6. A   7. C   8. B

1

CHAPTER 3: PUNCTUATION
Practice 1: End Marks
Pages 40–41
1. A   2. C   3. C   4. B   5. D

Practice 2: Commas
Page 42
1. B   2. C   3. D   4. A   5. D

Practice 3: Question Marks, Colons, and Apostrophes
Page 44
1. B   2. A   3. D   4. B   5. C   6. C

Practice 4: Sentence Types
Pages 46–47
1. B   2. C   3. D   4. C   5. C   6. A

Chapter 3 Review
Pages 48–50
1. D   2. B   3. D   4. D   5. B   6. A   7. A   8. C   9. A   10. D   11. A   12. D

CHAPTER 4: SPELLING
Practice 1: Spelling Rules
Pages 53–54 (top)
1. A   2. D   3. C   4. B   5. B   6. A

Practice 2: Homophones
Page 54
1. B   2. D   3. B   4. C   5. C

Activity: Homophones
Page 55
Responses will vary.

Chapter 4 Review
Pages 56–58
1. C   2. A   3. D   4. A   5. B   6. D   7. D   8. B   9. C   10. C

CHAPTER 5: WORKING WITH SENTENCES
Practice 1: Sentence Structure
Page 61
1. C   2. C   3. B   4. D   5. A   6. B

Practice 2: Using Varied Sentence Structure
Pages 63–64 (top)
1. C   2. B   3. A   4. D   5. A

Practice 3: Types of Sentences
Pages 64 (bottom)–65
1. A   2. A   3. D   4. B   5. C

Practice 4: Sentence Errors
Page 66
1. B   2. C   3. D   4. A   5. B

Chapter 5 Review
Pages 67–68
1. B   2. A   3. C   4. C   5. A   6. A   7. A   8. B   9. C   10. C   11. D   12. A

CHAPTER 6: WORKING WITH PARAGRAPHS
Practice 1: Revising Paragraphs
Pages 72–73
1. C   2. B   3. A   4. C   5. B   6. D

Practice 2: Organization
Pages 75–77 (top)
1. C   2. A   3. A   4. B   5. B   6. C

Practice 3: Main Idea
Pages 77 (bottom)–78
1. C   2. D   3. A   4. B

Chapter 6 Review
Pages 79–82
1. D   2. B   3. A   4. D   5. B   6. D   7. B   8. D   9. B   10. B   11. D   12. B

CHAPTER 7: WRITING ESSAYS
Practice 1: Essay Genres
Pages 85–86
1. B   2. D   3. A   4. C   5. D

Practice 2: Writing an Essay
Pages 89–90
1. B   2. D   3. A   4. C   5. C

Chapter 7 Review
Pages 91–94
1. B   2. A   3. A   4. C   5. A   6. B   7. C   8. D   9. A   10. C

CHAPTER 8: RESEARCH
Practice 1: Doing Research
Pages 98–100
1. B   2. C   3. D   4. A   5. B   6. C   7. A

Practice 2: Dictionary and Thesaurus Skills
Pages 102–103
1. A   2. B   3. A   4. C   5. A

Practice 3: Using Sources in Essays
Page 104
1. B   2. C   3. A   4. C   5. B

Chapter 8 Review

Pages 105–106

1. B   2. C   3. A   4. B   5. D   6. A   7. D   8. B   9. C   10. A   11. C

PRACTICE TEST 1

Pages 107–124

1. B	11. C	21. C	31. B	41. B	51. A
2. B	12. D	22. B	32. C	42. C	52. B
3. D	13. A	23. C	33. D	43. B	53. A
4. C	14. B	24. A	34. A	44. A	54. C
5. C	15. C	25. D	35. B	45. C	55. A
6. A	16. A	26. C	36. C	46. D	56. D
7. D	17. C	27. C	37. A	47. A	57. B
8. B	18. C	28. B	38. C	48. A	58. C
9. C	19. C	29. C	39. C	49. C	59. A
10. B	20. D	30. A	40. A	50. C	60. B

PRACTICE TEST 2

Pages 125–142

1. C	11. B	21. B	31. C	41. C	51. B
2. B	12. B	22. A	32. B	42. A	52. B
3. D	13. D	23. D	33. B	43. D	53. A
4. A	14. C	24. D	34. A	44. B	54. B
5. C	15. A	25. B	35. D	45. C	55. C
6. B	16. C	26. C	36. C	46. B	56. A
7. A	17. D	27. A	37. A	47. B	57. B
8. C	18. B	28. D	38. A	48. A	58. C
9. D	19. A	29. B	39. C	49. A	59. D
10. A	20. A	30. C	40. C	50. B	60. C

American Book Company
The Standards Experts

CRCT

Please fill out the form completely, and return by mail or fax to American Book Company.

Purchase Order #: _____ Date: _____ Contact Person: _____

School Name (and District, if any): _____ Phone: _____ Fax: _____

_____ E-mail: _____

Credit Card #: _____ Exp. Date: _____ Authorized Signature: _____

Billing Address: _____ Shipping Address: _____

Attn: _____ ☐ same as billing Attn: _____

_____ _____

_____ _____

Order Number	Product Title	Pricing* (10 books)	Qty	Pricing (30+ books)	Qty	Total Cost
GA1-M0809	Mastering the Georgia 1st Grade CRCT in Mathematics	$169.90 (1 set of 10 books)		$329.70 (1 set of 30 books)		
GA1-R0409	Mastering the Georgia 1st Grade CRCT in Reading	$169.90 (1 set of 10 books)		$329.70 (1 set of 30 books)		
GA2-M0409	Mastering the Georgia 2nd Grade CRCT in Mathematics	$169.90 (1 set of 10 books)		$329.70 (1 set of 30 books)		
GA2-R0409	Mastering the Georgia 2nd Grade CRCT in Reading	$169.90 (1 set of 10 books)		$329.70 (1 set of 30 books)		
GA2-H0409	Our State of Georgia (2nd Grade Social Studies)	$169.90 (1 set of 10 books)		$329.70 (1 set of 30 books)		
GA3-M0607	Mastering the Georgia 3rd Grade CRCT in Math	$169.90 (1 set of 10 books)		$329.70 (1 set of 30 books)		
GA3-R0607	Mastering the Georgia 3rd Grade CRCT in Reading	$169.90 (1 set of 10 books)		$329.70 (1 set of 30 books)		
GA3-S0508	Mastering the Georgia 3rd Grade CRCT in Science	$169.90 (1 set of 10 books)		$329.70 (1 set of 30 books)		
GA3-H1008	Mastering the Georgia 3rd Grade CRCT in Social Studies	$169.90 (1 set of 10 books)		$329.70 (1 set of 30 books)		
GA4-M0808	Mastering the Georgia 4th Grade CRCT in Math	$169.90 (1 set of 10 books)		$329.70 (1 set of 30 books)		
GA4-R0808	Mastering the Georgia 4th Grade CRCT in Reading	$169.90 (1 set of 10 books)		$329.70 (1 set of 30 books)		
GA4-S0708	Mastering the Georgia 4th Grade CRCT in Science	$169.90 (1 set of 10 books)		$329.70 (1 set of 30 books)		
GA4-H1008	Mastering the Georgia 4th Grade CRCT in Social Studies	$169.90 (1 set of 10 books)		$329.70 (1 set of 30 books)		
GA5-L0210	Mastering the Georgia 5th Grade CRCT in ELA	$169.90 (1 set of 10 books)		$329.70 (1 set of 30 books)		
GA5-M0806	Mastering the Georgia 5th Grade CRCT in Math	$169.90 (1 set of 10 books)		$329.70 (1 set of 30 books)		
GA5-R1206	Mastering the Georgia 5th Grade CRCT in Reading	$169.90 (1 set of 10 books)		$329.70 (1 set of 30 books)		
GA5-S1107	Mastering the Georgia 5th Grade CRCT in Science	$169.90 (1 set of 10 books)		$329.70 (1 set of 30 books)		
GA5-H0808	Mastering the Georgia 5th Grade CRCT in Social Studies	$169.90 (1 set of 10 books)		$329.70 (1 set of 30 books)		
GA5-W1008	Mastering the Georgia Grade 5 Writing Assessment	$169.90 (1 set of 10 books)		$329.70 (1 set of 30 books)		
GA6-L0508	Mastering the Georgia 6th Grade CRCT in ELA	$169.90 (1 set of 10 books)		$329.70 (1 set of 30 books)		
GA6-M0305	Mastering the Georgia 6th Grade CRCT in Math	$169.90 (1 set of 10 books)		$329.70 (1 set of 30 books)		
GA6-R0108	Mastering the Georgia 6th Grade CRCT in Reading	$169.90 (1 set of 10 books)		$329.70 (1 set of 30 books)		
GA6-S1206	Mastering the Georgia 6th Grade CRCT in Science	$169.90 (1 set of 10 books)		$329.70 (1 set of 30 books)		
GA6-H0208	Mastering the Georgia 6th Grade CRCT in Social Studies	$169.90 (1 set of 10 books)		$329.70 (1 set of 30 books)		
GA7-L0508	Mastering the Georgia 7th Grade CRCT in ELA	$169.90 (1 set of 10 books)		$329.70 (1 set of 30 books)		
GA7-M0305	Mastering the Georgia 7th Grade CRCT in Math	$169.90 (1 set of 10 books)		$329.70 (1 set of 30 books)		
GA7-R0707	Mastering the Georgia 7th Grade CRCT in Reading	$169.90 (1 set of 10 books)		$329.70 (1 set of 30 books)		
GA7-S1206	Mastering the Georgia 7th Grade CRCT in Science	$169.90 (1 set of 10 books)		$329.70 (1 set of 30 books)		
GA7-H0208	Mastering the Georgia 7th Grade CRCT in Social Studies	$169.90 (1 set of 10 books)		$329.70 (1 set of 30 books)		
GA8-L0505	Passing the Georgia 8th Grade CRCT in ELA	$169.90 (1 set of 10 books)		$329.70 (1 set of 30 books)		
GA8-MATH08	Passing the Georgia 8th Grade CRCT in Math	$169.90 (1 set of 10 books)		$329.70 (1 set of 30 books)		
GA8-R0505	Passing the Georgia 8th Grade CRCT in Reading	$169.90 (1 set of 10 books)		$329.70 (1 set of 30 books)		
GA8-S0707	Passing the Georgia 8th Grade CRCT in Science	$169.90 (1 set of 10 books)		$329.70 (1 set of 30 books)		
GA8-H0607	Passing the Georgia 8th Grade CRCT in Georgia Studies	$169.90 (1 set of 10 books)		$329.70 (1 set of 30 books)		
GA8-W0907	Passing the Georgia Grade 8 Writing Assessment	$169.90 (1 set of 10 books)		$329.70 (1 set of 30 books)		

1-1-11 *Minimum order is 1 set of 10 books of the same subject.

American Book Company • PO Box 2638 • Woodstock, GA 30188-1383
Toll Free Phone: 1-888-264-5877 • Toll-Free Fax: 1-866-827-3240
Web Site: www.americanbookcompany.com

Subtotal _____

Shipping & Handling 12% _____

Total _____

Call Toll-Free 1-888-264-5877 to ORDER and for FREE PREVIEW COPIES!